A STUDY ON ENERGY EFFICIENCY AND SECURITY FOR PERVASIVE HEALTHCARE SYSTEMS

FEBRUARY 2017

ACKNOWLEDGEMENT

I wish to record my deep sense of gratitude and profound thanks to my research supervisor **Dr. P. Devaraj**, Assistant Professor, Mathematics Department, Anna University, Chennai, for his keen interest, inspiring guidance, constant encouragement and patience throughout my research period. Without him, I would not have been able to bring this thesis into fruition.

I am extremely indebted to my Doctoral Committee Members **Dr. Arul Siromoney,** Professor, Deparment of CSE, Anna University, Chennai and **Dr. S. Palanivel,** Professor, Department of Computer Science and Engineering, Annamalai University, Chidambaram, for their prompt help in providing excellent directions to do this research work.

I also thank **Dr. S. Swamynathan**, Associate Professor, **Dr. A. Kannan**, Professor, Department of IST, **Dr. P. Vivekanandan**, Professor, ACTech Campus, Department of Chemical Engineering, and **Dr. M.Chandrasekar**, Professor and Head, Department of Mathematics, Anna University, Chennai, for their valuable suggestions during the period of my research work.

I also thank my mother **Ms. S. Rajeswari**, who gave me support and wishes in doing this research work. I am indebted to my father **Mr. V. Sowrirajan(Late)**, who has been a source of inspiration throughout my life. I am grateful to my wife **Ms. K. Karthiga** and my son **Master. K. Ajay**, for their support and sacrifice during my research period. I also thank all my friends and relatives. Finally, I thank God for giving me opportunity to do this work by supporting wellness and blessings to me during my research period.

KANNAN S

TABLE OF CONTENTS

CHAPTER NO.		TITLE	PAGE NO.

LIST OF TABLES

LIST OF FIGURES

FIGURE NO.   **TITLE**   **PAGE NO.**

LIST OF ABBREVIATIONS

HEED	-	A Hybrid Energy Efficient Distributed Clustering
ANYBODY	-	A Self-organization Protocol for Body Area Networks
WAITER	-	A Wearable Personal Healthcare and Emergency Aid System
WHEATS	-	A Wearable Personal Healthcare and Emergency Alert and Tracking System
AMON	-	Advanced Care and Alert Portable Telemedical Monitor
ABP	-	Ambulatory Blood Pressure
ADC	-	Analog to Digital Convertor
A-GPS	-	Assisted Global Positing System
ANGELAH	-	AssistiNG ELders At Home
AIDC	-	Automatic Identification Data Collection
BP	-	Blood Pressure
BTU	-	British Thermal Units
CSMA	-	Carrier Sense Multiple Access
CDMA	-	Code Division Multiple Access
C4ISRT	-	Command, Control, Communications, Computing, Intelligence, Surveillance, Reconnaissance and Targeting
CIA	-	Confidentiality, Integrity and Authentication
DoS	-	Denial of Service
ECG	-	Electrocardiography
EEG	-	Electroencephalography
EMG	-	Electromyography

EHR	-	Electronic Health Record
EMR	-	Electronic Medical Record
EPC	-	Electronic Product Code
ER	-	Emergency Room
EEPSC	-	Energy Efficient Protocol with Static Clustering
E-LEACH	-	Energy Low Energy Adaptive Clustering Hierarchy
E911	-	Enhanced 911
EDGE	-	Enhanced Data rates for GSM Evolution
ETX	-	Expected Transmission Count
EREERA	-	Extended Reselection - based Energy Efficient
XML	-	EXtensible Markup Language
FDA	-	Food and Drug Administration
FDMA	-	Frequency Division Multiple Access
FLEACH	-	Fuzzy Logic Low Energy Adaptive Clustering Hierarchy
GPRS	-	General Packet Radio Service
GPS	-	Global Positioning System
GSM	-	Global System for Mobile Communications
HIPAA	-	Health Insurance Portability and Accountability Act
HF	-	High Frequency
IFF	-	Identity Friend or Foe
IOM	-	Institute of Medicine
IMHMS	-	Intelligent Mobile Health Monitoring System
IPDA	-	Intelligent Personal Digital Assistant
ICU	-	Intensive Care Unit
IoT	-	Internet of Things
J2ME	-	Java 2 Micro Edition

LEACH-FL	-	LEACH implementation using Fuzzy Logic
LEACH-C	-	LEACH with Centralized Clustering Algorithm
V-LEACH	-	LEACH with Vice-Cluster Head
LED	-	Light Emitting Diodes
LAN	-	Local Area Network
LEACH	-	Low Energy Adaptive Clustering Hierarchy
LF	-	Low Frequency
MSHM	-	Medical Server for Healthcare Monitoring
MAC	-	Medium Access Control
MEMS	-	Micro-electro-mechanical Systems
MPHASIS	-	Mobile patient healthcare and sensor information system
M-LEACH	-	Multihop-LEACH
MMS	-	Multimedia Messaging Service
NS2	-	Network Simulator 2
NBC	-	Nuclear, Biological and Chemical
SpO2	-	Oxygen Saturation
PAN	-	Personal Area Network
PEL	-	Personal Emergency Link
PEG	-	Personal Energy Generator
PS	-	Personal Server
PCG	-	Phonocardiography
PPG	-	Photoplethysmography or piezoplethysmography
PEGASIS	-	Power Efficient Gathering in Sensor Information Systems
QoS	-	Quality of service
RF	-	Radio Frequency
RFID	-	Radio Frequency Identification
RAM	-	Random Access Memory

ROM	-	Read only Memory
RBS	-	Remote Base Station
REERA	-	Reselection-based Energy Efficient Routing Algorithm
SCHSA	-	Senior Citizen Home Safety Association
SARS	-	Severe Acute Respiratory Syndrome
SMS	-	Short Messaging Service
SIM	-	Subscriber Identity Module
T-LEACH	-	Threshold based LEACH
TEA	-	Time and Energy aware routing protocol
TDMA	-	Time Division Multiple Access
TL-LEACH	-	Two-Level Hierarchy
UHaS	-	Ubiquitous Health-assistant System
UHF	-	Ultra High Frequency
US	-	United States
USA	-	United States of America
USART	-	Universal Synchronous/ Asynchronous Receiver/Transmitter
VCR	-	Videocassette recorder
WBSN	-	Wearable Body Sensor Network
W-LEACH	-	Weighted Low Energy Adaptive Clustering Hierarchy
WBAN	-	Wireless Body Area Networks
Wi-Fi	-	Wireless Fidelity
WIM	-	Wireless Identity Module
WSN	-	Wireless Sensor Networks
WORM	-	Write Once Read Many

CHAPTER 1

INTRODUCTION

This chapter emphasizes the significance and characterization of Pervasive Healthcare Systems.

1.1 INTRODUCTION TO PERVASIVE HEALTHCARE SYSTEMS

Traditional Healthcare Systems are facing challenges in various ways because of the aged population growth around the world. Healthcare services cost has been increasing because of an exponential increase in the number of aged people in developed countries. Increase in aged people population has created major challenges for policy makers, healthcare providers, hospitals insurance companies and patients. One of the biggest challenges in providing better healthcare services for increasing number of people is limited financial and human resources.

Mark Weiser, the father of the ubiquitous computing, stated 'the most profound technologies are those that disappear'. Pervasive computing is the computing that enters the physical world and bridges the gap between the virtual and physical world (Sanchati et al. 2011). Pervasive computing technologies used in healthcare research focus on the directions of pervasive, user-centred and preventive healthcare model. It does not aim to replace traditional healthcare. Pervasive healthcare technologies can be used in all stages of life to motivate healthy behavior and disease prevention compared to traditional disease treatment.

The advanced development in computing power, sensors, embedded devices, smart phones, wireless communications, networking, data mining technique, cloud computing and social networks have made researchers and practitioners to create pervasive computing systems that respond to users in context-aware and situation-aware approach automatically. Pervasive systems must be designed in such a way that it must be able to function over varied spatial and temporal scales and encompass a large number of computational platforms, users, devices and applications dealing with large amounts of data (Cook & Das 2012). Pervasive technology has wide area of applications, among them, the most important application is healthcare, including support for independent living and wellness and disease management. Pervasive healthcare has a mission of helping the patients to manage their own disease and communicate and collaborate among healthcare professionals.

According to the healthcare requirements, infrastructure should be developed in such a way that utilizes wireless technologies in an effective manner such as location tracking (Koshima & Hoshen 2000), intelligent devices, user interfaces, body sensors (Bhargava & Zoltowski 2003, (Lymberis 2003), and short-range wireless communications for health monitoring. To increase accessibility of healthcare providers, instant, flexible and universal wireless access can be used and for effective emergency management communication among medical devices, patients, healthcare providers and vehicle should be reliable. The current and emerging wireless technologies help in achieving quality of service to patients (Varshney & Vetter 2000), (Boric-lubecke & Lubecke 2002). By using these wireless technologies, we can reduce the stress and strain on healthcare providers thereby we can enhance their productivity, retention and quality of life, and reduce the long-term cost of healthcare services (Varshney 2005, 2006).

In future, affordability, portability, and reusability features of wireless technologies (Raatikainen et al. 2002) can help in reducing the overall healthcare services cost which include health monitoring and preventive care service cost (Schepps & Rosen 2002).

Devices or technologies used in pervasive healthcare systems are very limited in energy resources. So energy efficient is vital for these pervasive healthcare services. Energy efficiency techniques suitable for these applications must be combined and designed in such a way that it meets the demands of pervasive healthcare systems. Since Medical Data's are sensitive it should be prevented from malicious and unauthorized access or attacks. So security plays a vital role for pervasive healthcare services. Patient misidentification also leads to medical errors. By using pervasive healthcare systems this errors can be reduce.

In this thesis pervasive healthcare systems issues such as energy management in devices, security of medical data, identification of patients, accessing techniques of electronic health record and efficient resource management are addressed.

An important problem in wireless sensor network is that energy on network nodes is very limited. The maximum energy is lost by data transmission and communication. Hence, maintaining energy efficiency is required for increasing network lifetime. Clustering helps to solve this problem. LEACH is one of the clustering mechanisms which can help in prolonging the network lifetime. Reselection based energy efficient routing algorithm (REERA) is an improvement of LEACH. In this thesis work on Energy efficiency and load balancing in wireless sensor network used in wearable physiological monitors uses REERA and extended it and compared with LEACH, E-LEACH, W-LEACH, and LEACH-FL . Energy efficiency is still further enhanced by using min heap algorithm. Min heap algorithm is used for load balancing among cluster heads. Health care cost can be reduced by monitoring patient vital signs remotely and continuously. For patient, soldiers and athletes monitoring of human body and surrounding environment is important. WBAN and WSN application integrated approach can be used for continuous healthcare monitoring. Patient or solider fatigue can also be monitored by using this application.

Traditional healthcare system is unable to provide freedom and comfort to patients because of lack of monitoring setup. A novel Wearable Personal Healthcare and Emergency alert and tracking system, namely WHEATS is proposed in this thesis work. The proposed system gives flexibility to the users to move freely wherever they wish to go. In case of emergency user is tracked by WHEATS and treatment is given immediately so that user is safe.

WHEATS continuously collects personal health status and periodically sends the status reports to healthcare centre and rapidly issues the alerts for medical aid in case of emergency. Also it dials family members, friends, neighbor and ambulance number. Early diagnosis, disease prevention and medical decision can also be done effectively by using this proposed system. By using this system, there is an obvious benefit to the person to achieve an enhanced quality of life.

Patient safety is an important factor for quality of health care. "To Err is Human" (Kohn et al. 1999). Adverse events are third largest cause of death. An adverse event is any untoward medical occurrence in a patient or clinical investigation subject administered a pharmaceutical product and which does not necessarily have a causal relationship with this treatment. Adverse events appears during the prescription or validation or dispensation or administration of medication to the patient. Growth of wireless communication technologies changed the traditional healthcare monitoring setup to dynamic monitoring setup environment.

Radio Frequency Identification (RFID) is a wireless technology helps pervasive healthcare environment to perform various tasks such as identifying or tracking patients, reducing medical errors, reducing malicious attacks, measuring patient care and waiting times, monitoring doses of medication, ensure the correct matching between the patient and doctor.

(Karthikeyan & Sukanesh 2012) discussed about palm vein which is unique in nature. Nobody in this world has the same palm vein. There is no chance for duplication. It will not vary during the person's lifetime. It is a much secured method of authentication and verification because this blood vein pattern lies under the skin. This makes it almost impossible for others to read or copy.

Security of a tamper resistant prescription RFID access control system of earlier protocol is analyzed. Analysis shows that, since reader and tag are devices, there is a possibility for mishandling these devices. In earlier protocol only devices area authenticated not the user who is using or going to use. This leads to malicious attacks with the success probability as '1' and the complexity of the learning phase of the attack is only eavesdropping a part of one run of the protocol. Palm vein based protocol which is unique in nature is proposed in thesis work to maintain patient safety.

Medical data is very sensitive. So, there is need for tamper resistant prescription. Maintaining and carrying medical records are reduced for elders and patients by designing tamper resistant prescription RFID access control system. Hospital database server stores every medical record as electronic record. So by this way, paper records and paper usage are eliminated. Thus, hospital will be environment friendly.

A secured access method for establishing communication and key exchange method between two readers is proposed in this thesis work. The proposed protocol includes authentication mechanism and access right authorization mechanism and reader to reader communication using key exchange protocol. For example if a heart patient wants to be treated by a cardiologist, then the patient may be asked to consult subordinate (reader 2) for example, subordinates takes ECG and other tests related to the treatment and keeps all records ready and send it to the cardiologist(reader1). This shows the importance of reader to reader communication by using chaos based key exchange protocol.

This research work finally concludes the ways and means for accomplishing energy efficiency and security in pervasive healthcare systems. Indeed, by using Wireless Sensor Network, Wireless Body Area Network and Radio Frequency Identification, qualitative treatment to patients is ensured.

1.2   NEED FOR PERVASIVE HEALTHCARE SYSTEMS

In earlier days, family physicians through visits delivered medical care at home. (Arnrich et al. 2010) Physician had a doctor's bag which contains all the necessary medical technology in the bag. But in 20th century, it is very rare and very expensive these specialist and technologies should be centralized in hospitals to make their utilization effective (Koop et al. 2008). Today, hesalthcare systems are facing challenge in various ways due to ageing population. Challenges are: increase in chronic diseases and co-morbidity, medication side effects, compliance problems and lifestyle guidance among the elderly, and the need for long-term care and need for elderly people assistance (Codagnone 2009).

Dominant forces driving the future healthcare are predicted as increase in chronic disease conditions and age-related illnesses as discussed in (Kaye & Zitzelberger 2006). Healthcare systems should move to distributed networked healthcare systems from healthcare professional centric systems due to quality and cost issues. Also, an individual will become an active partner in the care process (Korhonen et al. 2003). Healthcare system should transform from managing illness to maintaining wellness (Dishman 2004). Pervasive technologies play a vital role in this transformation (Tröster 2005).

Pervasive computing technologies used in healthcare research focus on the directions of pervasive, user-centered and preventive healthcare model. It does not aim to replace traditional healthcare. The vision of user-centered preventive healthcare can be achieved by pervasive technology. Pervasive healthcare technologies can be used in all stages of life to motivate healthy behavior and disease prevention compared to traditional disease treatment.

1.3   REQUIREMENTS FOR PERVASIVE HEALTHCARE, ITS APPLICATIONS AND WIRELESS REQUIREMENTS

In recent years, interest in developing new sensing and monitoring devices, including wireless wearable mobile devices and sensing networks for medical health applications has been increased. Medical sensors developed nowadays are more intelligent, miniaturized, low power, multi-parameter, and noninvasive compared to traditional medical sensors (Ting & Yong 2016).

Wireless biomedical sensor must meet the requirements such as wearability, reliability, security and interoperability to provide efficient healthcare. Wireless sensor networks have many challenges among them energy, security and privacy seemed to be the major challenge (Issac & Enobong 2016).

At present, wearable smart vests and shirts, which are non-invasive, comfortable and convenient to wear and it also has the capability of detecting physiological signals such as ECG, EMG, BP, HR, BT, respiration, posture and activity to improve the accuracy of the patient diagnosis. There are some technological barriers such as the limitation of currently available battery technologies and energy scavenging, security of private information transportation, improvements in sensor miniaturization and efficiency.

Cultural barriers such as standardization and cooperation at all levels and clinical validation are to be considered for wearable medical monitoring system. Some of the systems are not perfect as expected. The price is relatively so high that common families could not be able to afford it, and the precision of some devices cannot satisfy our needs leading to misdiagnoses. Current status of developing integrated, reliable, cost-effective and user-friendly wearable medical systems is far from the goal of affordable, real-time, anywhere, high security and accuracy and clinical validation is also very important to achieve this goal.

Pervasive societal problem homelessness can be addressed by electronic healthcare technology. Mental illness a leading cause of homelessness and attention to the study of medication adherence within electronic healthcare research and systems dynamics model should be designed to address complex societal challenges and affordances during one time period can become constraints in another (Ahluwalia et al. 2015).

Mobile health (or m-health) helps in delivery of healthcare services using mobile technologies. Mobile technologies can be used for instant communications and access to healthcare professionals, and with access to multiple wireless networks, it can facilitate decision making process for emergency cases. The amount of traffic generated, transmitted over networks, and presented to healthcare professionals should be reduced without sacrificing the quality of information (Varshney 2014).

m-health highly dependent on sensors, mobile devices and wireless infrastructure. Hence, it cannot solve all problems of healthcare. Mobile health is not possible in places where there is no wireless coverage or when mobile devices have battery or access problems. Also, m-health cannot and should not completely automate the delivery of healthcare services. Human involvement is important for some of the m-health applications because of their potential for damage or injury to the patient's health. FDA has given some guidelines on mobile health applications. The FDA rules will not be applicable to application providing healthcare information which is not connected to any healthcare delivery device (Varshney 2014).

A communication between a patient and a healthcare professional is a critical requirement of comprehensive patient monitoring solutions which should be reliable in case of emergency transmissions. An unpredictable spotty network coverage of infrastructure based networks used for technology enabled patient monitoring must be fully resolved which can lead to negative impact towards the goal of remote patient monitoring applications. Mobile ad hoc network, formed among patient monitoring devices, has the capability to enhance network coverage and signal transmission from an area where low or non-existent coverage from infrastructure based networks (Sneha & Varshney 2013).

Pervasive healthcare must be designed according to (Varshney 2007) in a such way it should have high level of security, high level of privacy, devices should be portable, wireless infrastructure used should be reliable, accessible and usable, reducing healthcare cost by designing new business model and training and adoption should be done according to the

HIPAA in USA regulatory frameworks. Management challenges such as insure payments, liability and role and restrictions should be solved.

Applications:

A possible scenario like user's mobile device can store and update all the necessary medical information and critical information such as blood group, allergies and existing medical conditions to be delivered for emergency and correct medical care. In current and future, wearable and handheld devices can be used to sense one or more vital signs and transmit alert messages to healthcare providers, ambulance, car driver and hospital. It can also be used to save many lives by providing efficient vehicular routing and information to nearby hospital. So, patients can be treated immediately.

In another scenario, patient during normal checkup can upload the necessary medical and insurance information by using their handheld device to doctor's office. Therefore, amount of efforts and /or inconsistency in entering detailed information can be reduced.

Wireless and mobile technologies can provide several new healthcare applications. Some of these applications are as follows (Varshney 2014):

- Comprehensive health monitoring services can be used in monitoring patients at anytime and anywhere. Context awareness can be built in pervasive services to avoid "false-positive" alerts. By this way, time between the occurrence of an emergency and the arrival of need help can be reduced.

- Emergency Management System should be designed based on information from mobile and wireless networks. By adding intelligence to this system, it will be able to manage many calls received due to a single accident or incident and emergency vehicles are effectively managed.

- Health-aware mobile devices can be used to find patient's certain conditions by the touch. Within handheld wireless device some of the portable medical devices can be integrated. These devices can be very useful in detecting pulse-rate, blood pressure, and level of alcohol. Based on the known allergies and medical conditions, the device will alert healthcare emergency system (similar to enhanced-911 used in U.S.).

- Pervasive access anytime anywhere to healthcare information results in reducing number of medical errors. Healthcare provider or patient can access current and past medical information. Patients can restrict who can access their medical information and for how long. Healthcare decision makers can take better healthcare decisions with large amount of stored healthcare data in Mobile Healthcare Data Center. Healthcare researchers can do research on these data without identifying the patients.

- Pervasive lifestyle incentive management will allow money to be credited to user device every time when user does exercises or eats healthy food. This money can be used for mobile operator monthly payment or recharge. It can also be used for donating charity or for paying medical bills. This type of incentive can help individuals to lead healthy life and healthcare service cost can be reduced. This incentive management can be made available to everyone everywhere when wireless LANs supporting mobile payments deployed widely (Varshney & Vetter 2002),(Varshney 2003a).

Wireless requirements for pervasive healthcare services

Wireless networks used in pervasive healthcare services should have comprehensive coverage, reliable access and transmission of medical information, location management, and support for patient mobility. The wireless infrastructure should be designed in such a way it allows use of several diverse mobile and wireless networks to support the requirements of healthcare applications. It should also increase the access and quality of healthcare service by using location tracking, adhoc networking, and wireless network intelligence. The coverage and scalability challenges should be solved for wireless coverage in both rural and urban areas covering both indoor and outdoor environments.

Cellular networks can be combined with wireless LANs and it can be used to solve congested indoor and outdoor coverage problems in urban areas. In rural areas, coverage is very low or no coverage satellite and wireless LANs should be included in the infrastructure. By providing access to multiple wireless networks, coverage problems can be solved and the scalability of wireless infrastructure can be enhanced.

A comprehensive wireless architecture should be designed to track location. Location tracking can be done by using technologies such as GPS, E911 in cellular networks, wireless LANs, and RFID (Varshney, U 2003b). Location tracking has many benefits for healthcare applications such as tracking patients, tracking people with matching blood groups, locating organ donors, helping mentally challenged people and elderly people in hospitals and nursing homes.

ANNA UNIVERSITY, CHENNAI - 600 025

1.4   WIRELESS SENSOR NETWORK AND ITS APPLICATION IN HEALTHCARE

A wireless sensor network consists of a large number of spatially distributed devices called sensor nodes that are densely deployed inside the environment which we want to sense or close to it. Nodes are randomly deployed in inaccessible terrains or hazardous environments. A unique node called Base Station (BS) has more capability compared to all other nodes and nodes will send their data to Base Station either directly or through multi-hop communication (Amit et al. 2016). A Base Station may be either fixed or mobile node and provides wireless sensor network to connect it to the outside world. Sensor nodes components are shown in figure 1.1.

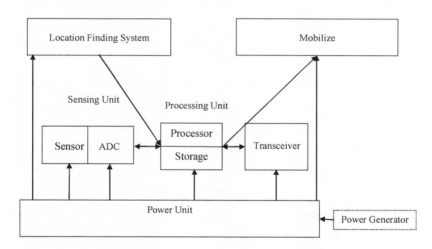

Figure 1.1 Sensor node components diagram (Akyildiz et al. 2002)

Figure 1.1 shows four basic components of a sensor node. They are a sensing unit, a processing unit, a transceiver unit and a power unit. Based on the application requirements, it can also have an additional component such as location finding system, power generator and mobilize. Sensing units are divided in to two subunits: sensors and analog to digital converters (ADCs).

Sensor node sensed data is analog signal that signal is converted to digital signals by the ADC, and then it is fed into the processing unit. The processing unit has a small storage unit and procedures that make the sensor node to collaborate with the other nodes and to carry out the sensing tasks which are assigned to them.

Network is connected by transceiver unit. Power unit is the most important component of a sensor node. Power units can also be supported by solar cells. Solar cells are examples for the techniques used for energy scavenging. Knowledge of location is very important for sensing tasks and routing techniques. Thus, sensor node should have a location finding system. All other subunits are application dependent.

A mobilize is needed to move sensor nodes when it is required to do the assigned task. Sensor nodes are inaccessible and the lifetime of a sensor network depends on the lifetime of the power resources of the nodes. Nodes are very small in size and it has very limited power resource in it. Nodes in a multihop adhoc sensor network plays dual role such as data originator and data router. Nodes which are not functioning will lead to topological changes, re-routing of packet and re-organization of the network. Hence, power conservation and power management are very important. Therefore, researchers are currently focusing on power-aware protocols design and efficient power saving algorithms for sensor networks.

Power consumption is categorized into three domains: sensing, communication, and data processing. Based on the nature of applications, sensing power will be different. Continuous event sensing requires more power compared to rare event sensing. Based on the event detection complexity, energy expenditure can be determined. Among the three domains, data communication uses maximum energy because data transmission and reception are involved in communication.

Medium access scheme used for sensor networks must support the operation of power saving modes for the sensor node. The most well known power conservation method is to turnoff the transceiver when it is not required further. This power saving method provides significant energy gain. By extracting energy from the environment (Rabaey et al. 2000) lifetime of the sensor networks can be extended.

Application of Wireless Sensor Network in Healthcare

The quality of care on different population can be improved through advances in medical sensors of WSN technology when applied in healthcare applications (Husnar & Ku 2016). Some of the healthcare applications using WSN to monitor special diseases like Parkinson (Jamthe et al. 2013), (Chakraborty et al. 2013), Alzheimer (Avvenuti et al. 2010) and heart attack (Jambhulkar & Baporikar 2015). An efficient WSN routing algorithm should provide high level of trustworthiness and ensure the security and privacy of the data for healthcare application (Ananthi et al. 2016), (Aminian & Naji 2013).

Isaac & Enobong (2016) discussed about how wireless sensor networks can be used in sampling of physical, physiological, psychological, cognitive and behavioral processes in spaces ranging from personal spaces to spaces within buildings and even larger scales. Some of the applications of WSNs include data mining for medical research, aged care, remote patients' monitoring, monitoring in mass casualty disasters, in-hospital vital signs monitoring, at-home monitoring, fall and movement detection and medication intake monitoring (Ko et al. 2010) ,(Alemdar & Ersoy 2010).

In recent years, Body worn sensors are coupled with internet enabled smart devices to have continuous collection of large chunks of medical data from a large distribution of subjects without distributing their daily lives. Computer assisted retrospective methods or replicated under controlled clinical and laboratory settings cannot measure subject state so they can make use of wireless sensor networks as an important tool in medical research (Ko et al. 2010).

When people become aged they have sensory and motor capabilities problems. At point of time they cannot take proper care of themselves and require assistance for their daily living. So there is an emergence of new intelligent assistive devices that gives information about a patient's physical and physiological states through sensors embedded in the device, worn or even implanted on the patient and the surroundings. A tag is placed on the user's hand. This tag helps to monitor which items the user picks and details are logged automatically on electronic daily activity forms. Health professionals can notice any deviations in the aged people activities by analyzing these forms (Alemdar & Ersoy 2010).

Wireless sensor networks help health workers with a means of monitoring patients both within and outside the hospital. In cases of mass casualty disasters the scalability and deplorability of wireless sensor systems can be an effective tool which can monitor continuously and automatically report the triage level of victims and the health status of first responders.

Traditional hospital vital signs monitoring has many bundles of cables or wires attached to the patients in hospitals in order to monitor their vital signs which causes discomfort like reduction in mobility and increase anxiety to the patients. Wireless sensor technologies address these drawbacks by eliminating the bundles of wires thereby mobility can be increased and in turn anxiety can be reduced. Wireless sensing hardware is less noticeable and maintains network connectivity with backend hospital systems in turn minimize occurrence of errors.

Patient suffering from conditions such as diabetes, asthma, congestive heart failure, obesity, chronic obstructive pulmonary disease and memory loss or decline may not necessarily have to stay in hospital. Wireless sensors embedded in or carried on patient suffering from these conditions are used to collect physical and psychological states of the patient in real time. Such data can also be used for early detection of diseases.

Alemdar & Ersoy (2010) discuss about leading cause of death among patients over 65 is accidental falls. Wireless sensor network can be used to prevent fall detection. (Wang et al. 2008) proposed a fall-detecting system by placing an accelerometer on the head level and using an algorithm to distinguish between falls and daily activities.

Elderly patient forget to take medication as and when due. Some of them refuse to do so. Wireless sensors can help in monitoring medication intake by patients. Pang et al. (2009) proposed a prototype ipackage which has the capability of performing both remote medication intake monitoring and vital signs monitoring. The ipackage controls dosage and uses RFID for identification of the correct pill.

From all the above work discussed the application of WSN in healthcare is justified.

PEER to PEER Communication

Wararkar et al. (2016) discuss about a peer to peer network is a part of highly distributed systems, contains a diverse number of nodes to form a network. These nodes are used to exchange content containing audio, video, data and various kinds of files without the use of a single server as in client server architecture. Such types of files make the network highly vulnerable. In the area of peer to peer security, there are five goals – Anonymity, Availability, File authentication, Access Control and Fair trading.

A peer-to-peer computer network refers to any network that does not have fixed clients and servers, but a number of peer nodes that function as both clients and servers to the other nodes on the network. Any node is able to initiate or complete any supported transaction. Peer nodes may differ in local configuration, processing speed, network bandwidth, and storage quantity (Agarwal et al. 2013). Many peer-to-peer systems are overlay networks that run on top of the internet (Schollmeier 2001).

Peer-to-peer systems have characteristics such as resource sharing, networked, decentralization, symmetry, autonomy, self-organization, scalable and stability. Attacks on peer to peer are such as network layer, overlay layer, application layer, interruption, interception, modification, fabrication, disruptive, degrading, passive and active attack. When no constraints are placed on who can join a peer to peer overlay, security problems can be created by any or all of the possibilities such as a new node supplying a legitimate nodeID but falsify-ing information in its own routing table, a new node supplying a fake nodeID that is meant to cause harm to the operation of the overlay, the same new node joining an overlay repeatedly with different nodeIDs and a set of nodes conspiring together with fake values for nodeID to disrupt the operation of the overlay (Agarwal et al. 2013).

Securing the peer to peer network has been an issue due to the lack of trusted managing authority and instability and further using it doesn't use Client Server Model so it requires more security features. In peer to peer network all the peers have equivalent authority and responsibility unlike the client server architecture. In client server architecture, the bandwidth usage of the main server keeps on increasing with the increase in number of clients. More the usage of bandwidth, lower will be the speed provided to the individual clients. Whereas in peer to peer, more the number of clients higher the download speed and less will be the usage of bandwidth as some part of bandwidth of each individual client is used.

WSNs can be hierarchical or distributed (flat) according to their network structure. In distributed network all sensor nodes communicate with the main station and the nodes which are in their range. On other hand, in hierarchical network, there are cluster of nodes where nodes can only communicate with their cluster heads and other nodes in the same cluster. This structure results in low communication cost. Hierarchical structure is more suitable for key distribution to reduce the communication cost.

The communication between sensor nodes in WSN is a type of peer-to-peer communication, since each node has the same capability and role. Security for networks is provided by cryptographic mechanisms such as encryption/decryption operations which are provided by public or symmetric key cryptography. Due to the limited battery power of nodes, symmetric key cryptography is used in WSNs. However, in symmetric key cryptography, it is not trivial to distribute these secret keys. In distribution, there is a trade-off between memory and resiliency. If only one pair wise key is used in whole network, it is obvious that it is not resilient to attacks. On the other hand, if different pair wise keys are generated for each pair, it is resilient to capture attacks (Kalkan & Levi 2014).

Peer to peer communication is needed in WSN to relay data to sink or healthcare center. So it is reasonable to allow peer to peer communication in healthcare applications but not directly before communication each node in peer to peer network should use some mechanism for secure communication because health data is sensitive and patient privacy is very important to be protected. These security problems can be prevented by introducing key mechanisms, user authentication, privacy protection, Data integrity, Access control, Usability, and Availability in each node participating in peer to peer network.

Every peer must prove its identity before joining the network mechanisms such as username and password or any other unique identifier can be used to prevent security attack. Real identity of the user should not be revealed. The data must be protected from any unauthorized access as the attacker can add malicious code that can modify the data or can even change the data completely. So data integrity feature deals with the genuineness of the data should be checked. By allowing access to only those users who have certain set of rights which makes them eligible to access the data. Interface should be user friendly so that it is very easy for user to understand and change the settings according to preferences. More complex interface might make user to choose setting which can become threat to the network. The data should be available to the authorized user whenever needs it.

The data being exchanged between the peers should be in the encrypted form. This can be done using cryptosystem. The keys used for encryption of data must be safely exchanged between the peers. Access control list which is object oriented that is, the user access is presented with respect to the object can be used to prevent the unauthorized access. Also, by using time stamp and the origin can help to manage the integrity of the file. Peers are assigned reputations and trust based on the content they provide and their behavior, a peer with less reputation will not be selected for download phase. These reputations scores are assigned by Reputation Computation Agent (RCA), so peer to peer network cannot be called as fully decentralized system. Each peer generates a public, Private key and shares it with the central RCA. RCA also has its own public and private key pair and it shares it public key with every peer registered in the network.

Within an Intranet multiple peers are connected to each other and they may exchange data with each other. For each Intranet there exists a Central Authority (CA) which monitors and checks the network and identifies any malicious activity. The whole Intranet is randomly scanned by CA for malicious data transmission and trace the peer who is sending the data and it will directly affect the reputation of the peer, so that the other peers don't download the data after an attack has been done by the provider. In this way the misuse of the reputation can be stopped. Any unusual behavior can be found by looking for a particular pattern in the network. If it finds something wrong in the network, it can immediately stop transmission of data so the uninfected peers could be saved.

The above discussion justifies peer-to-peer communication in WSN is reasonable with using additional security mechanism as mentioned as above.

1.5   WIRELESS BODY AREA NETWORK

Day-by-day so many innovations are made in healthcare for many developed nations because of the increase in average lifespan and health cost (Crosby et al. 2012). Advances in miniaturization of electronic devices, sensing, battery and wireless communication technologies developed wireless body area networks (wbans). Wireless body area networks (WBANs) are important branches of wireless sensor networks (WSNs).

WBANs are the extension of WSNs application (Xiaoling et al. 2014), but there are obvious differences between WBANs and WSNs (Table 1.1) (Aziz et al. 2006), (Raazi et al. 2010). They are used for patients'

health monitoring in real time and updates medical records which made attention in various fields. Smart miniaturized devices (motes) are included in WBANs which can do sensing, processing and communicating.

WBANs can be either worn or implanted, and task of WBANs is to monitor patient physiological signals without affecting their daily routine and transmit these signals to specialized medical servers for further analysis.

Security:

Security Requirements of WBAN

The WBAN and supporting infrastructure must implement security operations that guarantee the security, data integrity, privacy and confidentiality of the patients' medical records. In addressing privacy issues, it must be ensured that the Health Insurance Portability and Accountability Act of 1996 (Crosby et al. 2012) is observed.

The following security requirements must be attained (Crosby et al. 2012):

- Authentication

- Data Integrity

- Confidentiality

- Availability

- Privacy

In the Table 1.1 the difference between WBANs and WSNs are discussed. This table also shows challenges of both WBANs and WSNs.

Table 1.1 Difference between WBANs and WSNs

Challenges	Wireless Sensor Network	Wireless Body Area Network
Scale	Monitored environment(meters/kilometers)	Human body(centimeters/meters)
Number of nodes	Many redundant nodes for wide area coverage	Fewer, limited in space
Result accuracy	Large number of nodes provide accuracy	Few nodes, need to be robust and accurate
Node tasks	Node performs a dedicated task	Node performs multiple tasks
Node size	Small is preferred, but not important	Small is essential
Network topology	Very likely to be fixed or static	More variable due to body movement
Data rates	Most often homogeneous	Most often homogeneous
Node replacement	Performed easily, nodes are even disposable	Replacement of implanted nodes is difficult
Node lifetime	Several years or months	Several years or months, smaller battery capacity
Power supply	Accessible and can be replaced easily and frequently	Inaccessible and difficult to replace in an implantable setting
Power demand	Likely to be large, energy supply easier	Likely to be lower, energy supply more difficult
Energy scavenging source	Most likely solar and wind power	Most likely motion (vibration) and thermal (body heat)
Biocompatibility	Not a consideration in most applications	A must for implants and some external sensors

Table 1.1 (Continued)

Challenges	Wireless Sensor Network	Wireless Body Area Network
Security level	Lower	Higher to protect personal information
Impact of data loss	Likely to be compensated by redundant nodes	More significant, may require additional measures to ensure QoS and real-time data delivery
Wireless technology	Bluetooth, ZigBee, GPRS, WLAN, etc.	Low power technology required
Key management support from application	No	Yes, sensor nodes not required to generate random numbers
Human intervention	Not possible in most cases	Possible rather inevitable in some cases

Architecture of Ban

System architecture of wearable sensors for remote healthcare monitoring system (Gupta et al. 2012).

This system is composed of three tiers:

Wireless Body Area Network (WBAN)

Personal server

Medical server

First tier- WBAN is a collection of Wearable sensors which can be attached to the patient's body. WBAN monitors changes in patient's vital signs continuously and provides real time feedback to maintain an optimal health status.

Second tier- Intelligent Personal Digital Assistant (IPDA) collects physiological vital signs from WBAN user and processes the data. Also it prioritizes all the transmitted data based on the changes of vital signs of the patient and data content.

Third tier- Medical Server for Healthcare Monitoring (MSHM) receives data from Personal Server (PS) which is in medical centers. MSHM is capable of learning patient activity conditions and it learns from past medical history of the patient. Electronic medical records of the registered patients can be accessed through the internet by different medical staff, specialists and doctors. MSHM maintains theses Electronic medical records.

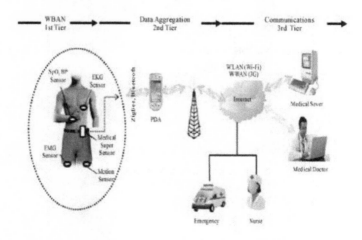

Figure 1.2 Architecture of BAN (Gupta et al. 2012)

Technical challenges of BAN are as follows (Ke & manmeet 2016):

- Power challenge

- Computational challenge

- Security and interference

- Material constraints

- Robustness

- Continuous operation

- Regulatory requirements

Ban Applications

A tiny wearable sensor helps in reducing the healthcare cost; it allows data collection automatically and reduces the inconvenience of the doctor's regular visit.

The various WBAN applications are as follows (Verma & Moinuddin 2014):

- Cardiovascular diseases prevention

- Cancer detection

- Depression and elderly people monitoring

- Glucose level monitoring reached

- Asthma

- HipGuard system

- MobiHealth

- LifeShirt

- eWatch

- Artificial Retina

- Military application

- Other applications

Energy Harvesting in WBANs

Sensor nodes used in WBANs are battery powered for its energy supply, but due to the size limitation of sensor nodes, battery cannot be big and so its lifetime is very short. It is difficult to maintain and replace it. Implanted nodes into the human body are directly related to power source of nodes (Guilar et al. 2006).

Environment where nodes are deployed will have all kinds of energy by using energy harvesting and storage unit's energy can be collected and stored for further processing. From the storage unit, energy can be transformed to the node when power is required by the node. By this way, long-term and effective energy supply is given to the node which is in need of power.

Battery Energy

WBANs sensor nodes are operated by battery power in it. These batteries have limited lifetime. So they can allow only very low energy consumption for tiny devices which leads to weaker processing capacity and less memory capacity for a while.

Battery revolution is very slow compared to the improvement of the mobile technology revolution. A small-sized rechargeable battery is used to achieve the network energy autonomy throughout the entire network lifetime.

Wearable medical devices are introduced in the thin-film and printed batteries (Imec & Centre 2011).

Solar Energy or Light Energy

Renewable and clean energy sources widely accepted is solar energy or light energy. The solar energy harvesting is done through photovoltaic conversion. Energy requirement of WBANs can be additionally supported by energy harvesting sources like solar energy or light energy. Since manufacturing costs of optoelectronic components can decline. This will be a reasonable good option for WBANs.

Cui et al. (2007) discussed that there will be heterogeneous nodes and their energy consumption and supply are different. When sunlight is not available, energy should be harvested from other sources also. Since it is bulky and rigid, it is difficult to wear in human body. So indoor photovoltaic energy harvesting is designed flexibly for wearable body sensor node (Toh et al. 2014).

Vibration Energy

To power the nodes, currently available potential energy is to use solar energy from a sun/light supply and followed by the design of vibration energy harvesters. Vibrations have sources of microenergy in the human body which can be derived from human motion during walking. Piezoelectric energy harvesting helps in converting mechanical vibration energy into electrical energy. There are many theoretical analyses and experimental measurements are available on mathematical modeling and piezoelectric energy converter applications (Roundy et al. 2003), (Lu et al. 2004), (Erturk & Inman 2008). (Anton & Sodano 2007) gave the application of ambient vibration research. Energy generated from the vibrating body is accumulated to power these nodes and it was used on animals (Philipp et al. 2012). Hip and foot instep is the most optimal point to place the device to collect the vibration-based energy harvesting and to generate energy efficiency and wearability (Olivares et al. 2010).

Thermal Energy

Thermoelectric generation is also energy harvesting solution. Also, from human warmth thermal energy can be harvested and that energy can be powered to the sensor node. Based on the amount of muscular activity energy will be released. These devices using Seebeck effect converts heat energy directly into electrical energy through its thermocouples. Since this energy source is unique, very small, and compact, it must be stored in a rechargeable battery or supercapacitor. (Hoang et al. 2009) discussed energy harvested by thermoelectric generator can be stored in an energy storage device.

Others

The human body itself is a very good source of energy. It can produce different types of energy, such as thermal energy, chemical energy, and kinetic energy. By human daily life activities, these energies can be generated from the body's own energy. Then, it can be converted to electrical energy through some kinds of devices. (Jamal et al. 2013) discussed the effective way of producing usable electric power from the sound energy. Piezoelectric microphones and piezoelectric pickups can produce electricity. Biological catalyst fuel in which the body's glucose will be breaking down from that energy is generated and sensor node gets power supply from it (Sasaki & Karube 1999).

Hybrid Energy

WBANs data is very sensitive and very important; so energy source is very important for communication, data transferring and data collection. Single energy source is not sufficient and reliable for energy harvesting. So, there is need for hybrid energy harvesting system. In order to obtain energy as much as possible for all kinds of energy from the environment should be collected by hybrid energy harvesting system. For indoor wireless sensor nodes, energy harvesting can be done by the solar and thermal energy system (Tan & Panda 2011). The mechanical harvesting system and piezoelectric harvesting system were designed in shoes whenever walking activity occurs electricity will be generated (Wei & Ramasamy 2011).

1.6 RADIO FREQUENCY IDENTIFICATION

Table 1.2 The decades of RFID (Roberts 2006)

Decade	Event
1940-1950	Radar refined and used, major World War II development effort. RFID invented in 1948.
1950-1960	Early explorations of RFID technology, laboratory experiments.
1960-1970	Development of the theory of RFID. Start of application field trials.
1970-1980	Explosion of RFID development. Tests of RFID accelerate. Very early adopter implementations of RFID.
1980-1990	Commercial applications of RFID enter mainstream.
1990-2000	Emergence of standards. RFID widely deployed. RFID becomes a part of everyday life.

Ernst Alexanderson in 1906, showed how the first radio wave could be generated continuously and how radio signals could be transmitted (Landt 2005). During World War II, the British wanted to know their own returning aircrafts and their enemy. Table 1.2 discusses the development of RFID in detail. To find their enemy, they placed transponders on their aircrafts which respond appropriately to interrogating signals from the base stations. This was called the Identity Friend or Foe (IFF) system and this was widely accepted as the first use of Radio Frequency Identification RFID (Domdouzis et al. 2007).

The main advantages of RFID over barcodes are as follows (Ahmad & Feng 2012):

- Line of sight is not required.
- Rugged.
- Reading speed is very fast.
- Read and write capacity based on the design allowed.
- Attaching it to outside the products is not necessary.
- Gives more flexibility.
- Data storage is high.
- Data collection throughput is increased.
- Data accuracy is good.
- Durability (works well even if it is dusty).

Components of RFID System:

A typical RFID system consists of three components as follows:

- RFID tags are called as transponder, tag is affixed to the object and that object can be recognized by this tag. Tags can be classified as active or passive tag. Battered tag is called active tags and from the environment or reader it takes power and it does not require power source which is called passive tags.

- A reader is called transceiver which is a powerful device with in-built memory. RFID reader has two interfaces. RF interface is the first interface which communicates with tags in their interrogation zone and communication interface is the second interface which interacts with the server.

- There is an application or data processing sub-system, which can be an application or database server depending upon the application design.

Table 1.3 discusses the difference between active and passive tags in detail.

Table 1.3 Difference between Active and Passive Tags (Ahmad & Feng 2012)

Factors	Active tag	Passive tag
Power	Internal	External
Life	Low	High
Transmitter	Yes	No
Cost	Expensive	Cheap
Read Range	(60-300)feet	Up to 30 feet
Data Storage	High	Less
Size	Slightly Bulky (Due to battery)	Small/light weight
Magnetic Field Strength	Low	High

RFID Communication Principal:

Magnetic or electromagnetic coupling is used for RFID communication. The difference between these two systems lies in their operating field.

Table 1.4 shows difference between Magnetic and Electromagnetic coupling system in detail

Table 1.4   Difference between Magnetic and Electromagnetic coupling system (Ahmad & Feng 2012)

Magnetic Coupled System	Electromagnetic Coupled System
Operate in LF or HF band	Operate in UHF and microwave band
Passively Operate	Active
Transformer Type Coupling	Backscatter Coupling
Using Amplitude Modulation	Using RF Power Transmission
Low Range	High Range

Deployment of RFID in Healthcare

Medical error is a very important issue in healthcare and so patient safety must be ensured. Radio Frequency Identification (RFID) is used in healthcare during medical procedures is to identify patients. However, based on the environment, data reliability and signal loss, RFID data readability will be better (Cheng & Chai 2012).

According to an Institute of Medicine (IOM) report, every year 44,000 to 98,000 people are dying due to medical errors which can be prevented (Kohn et al. 1999). During the course of healthcare delivery, there is possible for various types of medical errors such as improper transfusions, wrong-site surgery, and mistaken patient identities. Intensive care units, such as operating rooms and emergency departments are having high-error rate of chances for medical errors occurrence (Cheng & Chai 2012). Medical errors in these units will create serious consequences and many of these errors can be eliminated by proper design and error-proofing of the associated workflow.

When there are a large number of steps involved in medical process, there is a possibility for skipping or omitting unintentionally one or more steps, which is the most common error done by humans (Reason 2002). Before any medical procedures, most important process to be performed is patient identification. Errors in this process result in unrecoverable medical accidents and there are many medical accidents reported (Chassin & Becher 2002), (Jeon et al. 2009).

Currently, medical systems are using RFID in medical procedures, in order to monitor patients' safety(Jeon et al. 2009). RFID technology can be used to resolve the occurrences of patient misidentification (Murphy & Kay 2004), (Fisher 2006). It can also be used for institutes of medicine tracking records, management of medical materials and personnel. Since managing and handling great amounts of medical resources in institutes involves different floors or buildings, RFID is very suitable for such situations (Cheng & Chai 2012).

Hospitals can also use RFID with medical information system to improve tracking management of patients, medical resource, medicine, and storage, as well as elevating the quality of medicine (Ting et al. 2011). Currently, some hospitals have already accepted RFID for applications like operating rooms, Emergency Room(ER), newborn identification, and chemo medicine management, *etc.,* (Solanas & Castella-Roca 2008). Taipei Medical University Hospital in Taiwan is already using RFID for managing blood bag (Shang-wei et al. 2006).

RFID can be used for many areas like access control security management, goods-tracking management, implanting chips into animals, medical control applications, and logistics supply for American troops in Iraq wars because of their wireless in nature (Bansal 2003).

In medicine, hospitals should have more than two identification mechanisms to avoid wrong medicine or wrong transfusion to patients (Joo-Hee et al. 2005). RFID is used to identify patient accurately. Babies can wear RFID tags on their ankles or wrists to identify their mothers; and hospitals each entrance and exits have an electronic monitoring system set up by using RFID identification illegal carrying out of new born babies outside the hospital can be prevented.

RFID is a wireless sensor technology which is based on the detection of electromagnetic signals (McCarthy et al. 2003). RFID system consists of three components: an antenna or coil, a transceiver (with decoder) and a transponder (RF tag) which is electronically programmed with unique information. Antenna emits radio signals in order to activate tag and read and write data.

Communication between the tag and the transceiver is possible because of antennas. In order to become a reader, the transceiver and decoder are packed with antenna. The reader can be handheld or a fixed mounted device. Emission of radio waves from the reader can reach up to 100 feet or more, depending on its power output and the radio frequency used. Antenna produces electromagnetic zone if RFID tag is present in that zone, it detects the activation signal of the reader. Then, the reader decodes the tag data which is encoded in the integrated circuit of the tag and the data can be transferred to any computer system for further processing (Domdouzis et al. 2007).

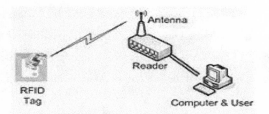

Figure 1.3 RFID components diagram

Figure 1.3 shows components of RFID and communications among them.

Tags can have read only memory (ROM), volatile read/ write random access memory (RAM) or write once/read many memory (WORM) in it. ROM is used to store security data and it can be used as a unique device identifier and in it, operating system instructions can be stored. RAM can be used to store transponder interrogation and response data in it.

Data contains a unique identifier which may also include:

- An operating system;

- Data storage (volatile or non-volatile); and

- An electronic product code (EPC – which is the successor of the bar code).

RFID in healthcare service sector

RFID technology has many application areas in the healthcare service sector day-by-day; their needs are growing exponentially, and some of them are door security, patient ID, inventory management, medical file management, pharmaceutical security, high-heat and sterilization, high accessibility, scalability, availability, error reduction at point of care, medications management, and real-time asset and employee tracking (Oztekin et al. 2010). Among the above mentioned applications possible usage of RFID systems in healthcare is tracking of critical assets which can be a shared resources leads to RFID usage in medical settings (Ngai et al. 2007), (Tu et al. 2009).

The location of the medical assets changes arbitrarily and continuously because of healthcare facilities in nature they are very complicated and unpredictable (Østbye et al. 2003). Therefore it should be tracked with RFID. Healthcare system performance depends on tracking mobile and highly critical medical equipment has highest priority compared to other factors. Many hospitals every year lose equipment such as infusion pumps, portable X-ray machines and patient monitoring devices and other assets such as wheelchairs, stretchers and gurneys, which cost from hundreds to thousands of dollars (Tzeng et al. 2008). Also spending precious time in searching these temporarily lost assets for patient care is ridiculous.

Central equipment supply staffs in the hospital spend hours perform a round-up each day to find equipment if there is no asset tracking system in the hospital. Manual searching in every department for unused equipment or equipment that requires servicing is a time consuming process and tedious one (Lee et al. 2008). Also, in order to increase timeliness of their services hospitals are overspending on additional assets which may lead to many high-value assets to be underutilized (Tzeng et al. 2008).

Deploying RFID in healthcare sectors, healthcare community are benefited by item tracking and security along with maintaining the highest level of data integrity (Paul 2004). While identifying and tracking objects, people in the hospital environment have many obstacles. It also creates difficulties in making real-time decisions such as different departments that use some assets as common, locating the assets in various local storage locations, locating healthcare providers and following patients' recovery trends (Avison & Young 2007).

In order to address identifying, tracking objects and people issues, (Li et al. 2004) proposed an integrated mobile healthcare service system which reduces the tracking time and increases the accuracy of positioning and identifying people with infection of SARS disease. (Wu et al. 2005) analyzed RFID based healthcare system which can identify the patient and compare drugs taken by them. This system helps the healthcare providers to eradicate patient-drug mismatches, over dosages and drug errors. (Booth et al. 2006) discussed other possible applications in the staffs and patients location such as theft prevention, patient safety, incident audit trail, dynamic patient-equipment association, equipment status, and cost capture.

RFID readers when placed throughout the hospital will reduce the search time for critical assets and less number of staff is required to perform the round-ups. Since the equipment locations are known and are accessed more rapidly, system will respond very fast and fulfill the patient requirements (Lee et al. 2008). Hence, RFID systems help nurses by reducing the searching time of equipment in an emergency situation and prevent materials managers from ordering excess number of equipments (Ngai & Riggins 2008). RFID based asset tracking system installed in hospital environment is very cost effective and it is economically justifiable (Chakrabarty et al. 2002).

RFID use in healthcare for asset tracking

According to (Lee et al. 2008) developed countries, economies are expanding towards the service industry and service orientation gradually shrinking on the manufacturing base. Currently, compared to all service industries, the healthcare sector is the fastest growing and the most critical due to the fact that it deals with human life and any deficiency in this sector can create inevitable and incurable results (Kaplan 1987). An unpredictable service demand and the complex infrastructure of hospitals, and finding the critical assets location quickly will be problems in the healthcare service industry (Lee et al. 2007).

For example, consider the scenario where an intensive care unit (ICU) nurse is using an oxygen regulator with a stable patient and is called up to help in an emergency case. Nurse must go immediately and take care of the patient than taking the oxygen regulator to its regular storage location. If the same oxygen regulator is needed by another nurse or doctor, locating that asset in a timely manner is difficult because it is not in its regular location, but in the ICU room where it was previously left. Therefore, medical assets tracking and information sharing of assets in real-time plays a very important issue. Hence, in absence of tracking these critical assets will result in poor service quality, low patient satisfaction, customer churn, loss of revenue and, more tragically, and even loss of the life of a patient (Kaplan 1987).

Quality of health care is affected by patient safety. There is no one method which guarantees a total absence of errors (Pérez et al. 2012). Also challenges faced by health professionals are occurrence of adverse events which should be reduced. It requires continuous tracking of the patient by different areas and services, a process known as traceability and proper patient identification and medication prescribed. RFID technology is used to perform various tasks such as locating the patients in different areas, measuring patient care and waiting times, identifying doses of medication, and ensuring the right doctor prescription medication for right patient.

Nowadays, maintaining a high level of safety in health care environments is a difficult task for which patient should be closely monitored from their arrival to discharge throughout their stay in the hospital. Also, task such as registering, administering, waiting and care times as prescribed and pharmaceuticals should be done accurately. This process is called as patient traceability which can contribute to guarantee the patient's own safety.

Patients should be identified and located at all times and that should be informed to their relatives or careers in real time of their clinical situation. Traceability application benefits the hospitalized patients which largely reduces the adverse events. Adverse event is any situation causing harm during the treatment process which is not related to the "base" illness of the patient and can lead to harm or even loss of life. According to (Andrés et al. 2005), 38% of adverse events appear during the prescription or validation or dispensation or administration of medication to the patient. In this process, all types of medical personnel are involved and their tasks are separated as doctor prescribes medication, pharmacist checks prescription and dispenses medication and nursing staff gives that medication to the patient.

According to (Kohn et al. 1999), "To Err is Human". A study related to adverse events at an international level shows their importance. Adverse events are the third largest cause of death and one in eight million probability of risk of death in an air accident while the mortality rate is one in every 550 hospitalizations. Further studies show that the countries such as Canada, New Zealand *etc* are also having this problem. Also, in Spain, studies show occurrence of this subject.

The success of RFID technology depends on large capacity that the labels should have to store information for identifying the subjects or objects that carry them. According to the standards, these data can be coded and stored. The labels are not damaged by usage, and it can withstand extreme temperatures and without direct contact with the reader hundreds can be read or written simultaneously. These properties make RFID an ideal technology for using in traceability systems which is very important requirement of healthcare environments like hospital centers or small scale like in units or services, and Emergency services.

1.7   ISSUES IN PERVASIVE HEALTHCARE SYSTEMS

- Energy management in devices

- Privacy of patient

- Security of medical data

- Validation of technologies and hypothesis

- Identification of patients

- Accessing techniques of electronic health record

- Noise in sensed data

- Delivery of timed intervention

- Efficient resource management

- Context awareness

1.8   OBJECTIVES OF THE THESIS

Some major issues from the list mentioned above are identified and are addressed in the thesis. They are listed below as main objectives of the work:

- To achieve energy efficiency and improve load balancing in wireless sensor network used in wearable physiological monitors.

- To design a model that is used to track a patient during emergency as a proof of concept.

- To ensure a secured access method while accessing patient electronic health record.

- To ensure a secured access method, establish communication and propose a key exchange method between RFID Multiple readers.

1.9 ORGANISATION OF THESIS

Chapter 1 presents the introduction to the Pervasive Healthcare Systems and its characteristics, the issues and challenges and also the objectives of this research work.

Chapter 2 discusses the various existing related research works with respect to the work presented in this thesis.

Chapter 3 deals with energy efficient and load balancing for wireless sensor network used in wearable physiological monitors.

Chapter 4 describes emergency alert and tracking system for wearable personal healthcare.

Chapter 5 describes a secure tamper resistant prescription RFID access control system.

Chapter 6 discusses a secure reader to reader communication protocol.

Chapter 7 discusses conclusion and future enhancements followed by references and publications.

CHAPTER 2

LITERATURE SURVEY

In this chapter some of the work which are related to the thesis work such as WSN, Personal Healthcare and RFID are discussed even though lots of articles are available in this field.

2.1   WSN

Design requirements for energy efficient schemes in WSN are Data collection and aggregation, Clustering and Routing (Sarika & Rama 2016). Data aggregation protocols are classified into two groups such as structure-free (Flat Network) and structured (Hierarchical Network) data aggregation protocols.

Fan et al. (2007) proposed a structure-free event-driven reporting scheme Data-aware anycast and randomized waiting for data aggregation in wireless sensor networks. A randomized waiting scheme is set up so that each sensor nodes after its random waiting time node which has to report event data can start its transmission. Aggregation efficiency is poor if the randomized waiting time selected by the sensor nodes nearer to base station is shorter.

Kulik et al. (2002) discussed about sensor protocol for information via negotiation. In this scheme, each sensor node requires the knowledge of its single hop neighbors only. But it is unable to guarantee data delivery. Chao & Hsiao (2009) discussed a technique structure-free and energy-balanced data aggregation for wireless sensor networks. This technique has efficient data gathering and balanced energy consumption, two-phase aggregation process and dynamic aggregator selection mechanism. But it has computation overhead while selecting dynamic aggregator and network holes are created.

Sardouk et al. (2010) proposed multi-agent data aggregation mechanism for structure-free event-driven wireless sensor networks. Inter-sensor-nodes redundancy is eliminated by co-operating agents and combines processed information of a gathered session into one message. Aggregator node is selected on the basis of event detection.

Boughanmi et al. (2013) have proposed energy efficient data aggregation mechanism in which sensor node which is aggregating and transmitting the concise message to the base station is selected on basis of its residual energy and proximity to the base station. Aggregator node which is selected on the basis of highest residual energy may not have sufficient energy for transmission to base station.

Distributed energy-balanced unequal clustering is proposed by (Jiang et al. 2012). In this mechanism an energy-aware multi-hop routing is adopted for inter-cluster traffic, to reduce and balance the energy overhead of the cluster heads. Unequal clusters may result in loss of information and full coverage problem. (Liao et al. 2013) proposed distributed self-organization balanced clustering algorithm in which communication costs are decreased as cluster head gathers the weight of all member nodes, and then selects the node with highest weight as the next head node. Random selection of trigger node for cluster head selection and energy holes may be created in this mechanism.

Chen (2013) proposed sink mobility based and energy balancing unequal clustering protocol in which cluster heads are the sensor nodes having higher residual energy and powerful communication capabilities. Non uniform energy drainage across different sensors may occur in this mechanism. (Xie & Jia 2014) proposed transmission-efficient clustering method which has optimal size of clusters based on number of transmission and compressive sensing is deployed to reduce redundancy. Coverage problem as some nodes may not join any cluster.

Sarika & Rama (2016) discussed about clustering challenges such as grouping adjacent sensor nodes and how many groups should be there that could optimize some performance parameter, determining optimal value of distance d that minimizes overall energy consumption, amount of data to be transferred within each cluster and between clusters, and selection of cluster head (CH) of a cluster.

In the year 2000, (Heinzelman et al. 2000) have developed LEACH (Low-Energy Adaptive Clustering Hierarchy). LEACH is a self-organizing, adaptive clustering protocol that uses randomization to distribute the energy load evenly among the sensors in the network.

Deployed nodes will organize themselves into local clusters with one node cluster-head. Conventional clustering algorithms have cluster head chosen before and fixed throughout the system lifetime. This leads to unlucky sensors chosen to be cluster-heads would die quickly. So, it will end the useful lifetime of all nodes belonging to those clusters. To solve this issue, LEACH uses randomized rotation of the high-energy cluster-head position such that it rotates among the various sensors in order to not drain the battery of a single sensor. Also, LEACH performs local data fusion to "compress" the amount of data being sent from the clusters to the base station. It also reduces energy dissipation and enhances system lifetime.

In LEACH, at any given point of time node with high energy has more probability to elect as cluster head (Heinzelman et al. 2002). All the cluster-head nodes will broadcast their status to the other sensor nodes present in their network. Based on minimum communication energy requirement, all sensor nodes decide to choose the cluster-head to which cluster they can attach. After all the nodes are organized into clusters, cluster-head creates and sends schedule to nodes which is in its range. Hence, non-cluster-head node can turn off their radio components except during their transmission time. By this way, energy is saved in the individual sensors.

After collecting data from its cluster nodes, cluster head node aggregates the data and then transmits the compressed data to the base station. Normally, the base station will be far away from the experimental location which requires high energy transmission. However, since there are only a few cluster-heads used it will only affect a small number of nodes.

LEACH is a popular clustering technique that forms clusters by using a distributed algorithm. It minimizes energy dissipation in sensor networks. There are many features of LEACH some of them are Localized coordination and control for cluster set-up and operation, randomized rotation of the cluster-heads and the corresponding clusters and local compression to reduce global communication.

By using clusters transmitting data to the base station requires only a few nodes to transmit which leads to energy saving. Compared to classical clustering algorithms, LEACH uses adaptive clusters and rotating cluster-heads, and distributes energy among all the sensors. LEACH before transmitting data to the base station does local computation in each cluster. Therefore, the amount of data to be sent is reduced which in turn reduces energy dissipation and computation is much cheaper than communication.

However, the main disadvantage of this approach is that a node with very low energy may be selected as a CH which may die quickly. Therefore, a large number of algorithms have been developed to improve LEACH such as PEGASIS (Lindsey & Raghavendra 2003), HEED (Younis & Fahmy 2004), EEPSC (Zahmati et al. 2007) *etc.* A number of clustering algorithms for WSN have been addressed in (Abbasi & Younis 2007), (Boyinbode et al. 2010), (Jiang et al. 2009) etc.

Compared to LEACH, PEGASIS improves network lifetime, but it requires dynamic topology adjustment and the data delay is significantly high and it is unsuitable for large-sized networks. (Kuilab & Jana 2012) proposed an algorithm of execution time O(n log n), in which no energy consumption issue has been addressed in this algorithm.

LEACH is a totally distributed approach and requires no global information. There are several modifications of the LEACH scheme, and together they form the LEACH family, such as Two-Level hierarchy LEACH (TL- LEACH) (Loscri et al. 2005), Energy- LEACH (E- LEACH) (Akkaya & Younis 2005), Multihop- LEACH(M- LEACH) (Akkaya & Younis 2005), LEACH with Centralized clustering algorithm (LEACH-C) (Liu 2012), LEACH with Vice-cluster head (V- LEACH) (Yassein et al. 2009), LEACH implementation using Fuzzy Logic (LEACH-FL) (Kim et al. 2008), Weighted- LEACH(W- LEACH) (Abdulsalam & Ali 2013), Threshold based LEACH (T- LEACH) (Hong et al. 2009).

LEACH cannot provide actual load balancing. Cluster heads are elected only on the basis of probability, not taking energy into consideration and uniform distribution cannot be ensured. Thus, nodes with lower energy will be selected as cluster heads, which leads to death of these nodes very quickly. Reselection-based Energy Efficient Routing Algorithm (REERA) is an improvement of LEACH (Wang et al. 2013).

Weiya & Chao (2009) proposed integrated application of WBAN and WSN. In this work they have proposed a Gradient Routing Protocol for WSN which satisfied the needs of WBAN data transfer. (Maskooki et al. 2011) proposed an opportunistic routing scheme for WBANs. Body movements can increase lifetime of sensors by opportunistic routing protocol.

Khan et al. (2013) authors discussed three types of nodes based on their energies such as normal, advanced and super nodes. Super nodes have more energy compared to other two. So they are selected as cluster head. (Watteyne et al. 2007) proposed ANYBODY a clustering based protocol. Efficiency of network is increased by changing the selection criteria of cluster head.

Yu et al. (2010) discussed mobile sink in WSN which can improve network lifetime. Due to sink mobility, the dynamic topology of a WSN should be developed. (Chatzigiannakis et al. 2008) authors discussed predictable or fixed-path mobility pattern which gives detail about the expected time of visit of the mobile sink.

Hoang et al. (2009) discussed on thermal energy harvesting which can be used in WBAN Sensor nodes for battery charging. (Jain 2011) discussed about using solar energy for WSNs. Energy harvested is used to charge batteries of WSNs sensor nodes. (Olivares et al. 2010) discussed about vibration energy harvesting due to random motion of humans. This energy can also be used for charging batteries. (Khan et al. 2013) discussed about cluster based reactive routing protocol. In that cluster head is selected based on residual energy of nodes and average energy of the network.

Asha et al. (2016) discuss about security of wireless sensor network and how to protect the network from numerous attacks. Also, providing hundred percent securities and maintaining confidentiality is a huge challenge in recent trends. Nowadays wireless communication technique has become a very important tool in any application that requires communication between one or more senders and multiple receivers (Venkataraman et al. 2013). WSNs are vulnerable to security attacks because nodes are often deployed in a hostile or dangerous environment where they are not protected.

Basically the attacks are classified as passive and active. The monitoring and listening of the communication channel by unauthorized attackers are known passive attack (Kumar et al. 2014). The attacks against privacy are passive in nature. The unauthorized attacker monitors, listens to and modifies the data stream in the communication channel are known as active attack (Kumar et al. 2014). Passive attacker act as normal node and gathers information from WSN. Also does monitoring and eavesdropping from communication channel by unauthorized attackers.

Monitoring and eavesdropping is the most serious security threats to WSN. Eavesdropping can act effectively against the privacy protection (Kaur & Kaur 2014). Traffic analysis attack is after hiding information on a message the hacker is able to view the information it would traffic analysis attack. Sensor activities reveal the enough information to the intruder which they use to harm the network (Alam & De 2014). Camouflage adversaries intruder can insert their node or compromise the nodes to hide in the sensor network.

Passive attacks are very difficult to find out because an attacker does not modify the data, but monitor and eavesdrop to obtain the data. Sender or receiver is aware that an intruder or adversary or attacker has read the messages when messages are exchanged between them. Encryption technique can be used to prevent this type of attack.

Active attacker can perform operations such as injecting fault data into the WSN, impersonating, packet modification, unauthorized access, monitor, eavesdrop and modify resources and data stream, overloading the WSN. Attacker modifies the data from inside or outside the sensor network. Attacker out of the WSN's scope is an external attacker who does jamming the entire communication of the WSN and WSN's resource consumption. If the attacker is in the WSNs scope is an internal attacker who does revealing secret keys and partial or total degradation.

Attacker can involve in changing the routing information called routing attack. In Selective forwarding attacker forwards some selective packets. It is hard to figure out selective forwarding attack in sensor network. In Black hole (or sinkhole attack) attacker builds a covenant node which seems to very attractive in the sense it promotes zero cost routes according to routing algorithm (Singla & Sachdeva 2013) to neighboring nodes which results maximum traffic to flow towards this false node, to attract all the packets which are destined to the sink node. Nodes adjoining to this harmful node collide for bandwidth which results in resource contention and message destruction.

In wormhole attack, a pair of awful nodes creates a wormhole tunnel to replay the packets. Attacker node copies a portion or whole packet and speed up to send the packet the through the wormhole tunnel, so that the packets arrive first to the destination before the original packets traverse the usual routes. This may cause congestion and retransmission of packets squandering the energy of innocent nodes. False node is injection of malicious node into the network by an adversary is called false node. This malicious node feeds the false data into the network or avoids the passage of true data.

Denial of service is a simplest attack tries to exhaust the resources available to the victim node, by sending extra unnecessary packet and thus prevents legitimate network users from accessing services or resources to which they are entitled (Sharma & Ghose 2010). Physical attacks are more dangerous because they destroy the sensors permanently, where the losses are irreversible. So there are chances of losing the cryptographic secrets, tamper with the associated circuitry, modify programming the sensors or replace them with malicious sensors under the control of the attacker ((Alam & De 2014).

Data confidentiality is the most important issue in network security. Sensor nodes may communicate highly sensitive data, such as key distribution which leads to a secure channel in WSN (Chelli 2015). The principle of confidentiality specifies that only the sender and intended recipient should be able to access the contents of the message (Vani & Monali 2013). When the contents of the message are altered by an adversary before reaching the intended recipient integrity of the message is lost.

WSN having confidentiality measures also have possibilities for the data integrity could be compromised by alterations (Kumar et al. 2014). The integrity of the network will be problem when a malicious node present in the network injects false data. Any data before using in decision-making process should be verified where it comes from the correct source or not.

Authentication mechanism helps in identifying proof of identities, which ensures origin of message or whether document is correctly identified (Vani & Monali 2013). The principle of availability states that resource such as sink node should be made available to authorized parties at all times because failure of the sink node threatens the entire network.

Data freshness ensures that the data communicated was recent and no previous messages have been replaced by an adversary (Vani & Monali 2013). To ensure the freshness of a packet, a time stamp can be attached to it. Receiving node can compare the time stamp with its own time clock and checks whether the packet is valid or not.

A sensor network insists every sensor node to be independent and ductile enough to be self-organizing and self-healing according to different situations (Chelli 2015). There is no fixed infrastructure available for the network management, so nodes must themselves adopt the topology and deployment strategy. Secure localization's makes use of geological based information for recognition of nodes since some attacks work based on the location of the nodes. Sensors may get displaced while deploying them or after at time interval (Chelli 2015).

2.2   PERSONAL HEALTHCARE

Wearable medical monitoring systems based on wireless networks with emphasis on devices based on textile and wireless sensing networks. These monitoring systems consist of various types of small physiological sensors, transmission modules, and processing capabilities (Ting & Yong 2016). (Matzeu et al. 2016) used camera sensor to monitor sweat rates via image analysis. They have used smart phone micro controller hardware to monitor sweat. (Ning et al. 2016) designed electrocardiography monitoring system based on wireless communication.

A smart shirt consists of six electrodes is placed on the chest to measure a detailed electrocardiogram (ECG) obtained with unipolar precordial leads (Tada et al. 2015). Levels of mental attention can be monitored with a small number of non-gelled electroencephalogram (EEG) electrodes (Poltavski 2015). (Sandulescu et al. 2015) used electodermal sensor incorporated into a wristband to measure stress. (McCall 2015) ,(Chen et al. 2014) discusses the possibilities to identify the severity of depressive symptoms based on the number of conversations, amount of physical activity, and sleep duration using a wearable wristband and smartphone app. A microananalysis of body movement data can be used to detect early symptoms of Parkinson disease (Arora et al. 2014).

Smart phone healthcare monitoring system is designed to measure oxygen saturation and heart rate (Fang et al. 2014). Posture monitoring vest is designed and developed to monitor multi-posture, long time monitoring and emergency (Lin et al. 2014). BIOTEX (Coyle et al. 2010) and Proe-TEX(Curone et al. 2010) and AMON(Anliker et al. 2004) uses sensor-based and wirst-worn devices to measure various parameters such as sweat rate, respiratory activity, ECG and heart rate (HR). A wireless long-term health monitoring system with lower power consumption is developed by (Haahr et al. 2012) which has electronic patch to detect physiological parameters.

Magic system (Meriggi et al. 2010) measures physiological parameters such as ECG, SpO2, R and posture. Integrated sensors are ECG electrode and 3D-acceleration. It is used to monitor the climbers in a real-time while they are climbing the altitude on mount everest slopes. Bluetooth is used as communication medium along with PDA and vest with textile sensor.

Elite care (Wu et al. 2008) is a personal healthcare system based on a smart space, where the sensors and wireless communication devices are deployed unobtrusively. Elite care can only serve the people living in the specific smart space, which is costly and unlikely to be widely used. CodeBlue is an AdHoc Sensor Network Infrastructure for Emergency Medical Care (Malan et al. 2004). CodeBlue is designed just for emergency medical care and it cannot contribute to sickness prevention and early diagnosis.

Personal Emergency Link (PEL) system (Wu et al. 2008), established by Senior Citizen Home Safety Association (SCHSA), can provide emergency medical service for elderly or disabled people. PEL cannot keep track the patients' health situation and is unable to actively issue an alert if the patient is unconscious. AMON (Anliker et al. 2004) is an advanced care and alert portable tele-medical monitor (AMON), targeting at healthcare for high-risk cardiac/respiratory patients. The functions of AMON include continuous collection and evaluation of multiple vital signals, intelligent medical emergency detection, and a cellular connection to a medical centre. AMON needs to integrate the GSM module into it, which has not well used the commercial products of mobile phone and caused high cost.

WAITER (Wu et al. 2008) continuously monitors personal body status in a real-time manner and automatically issues the alert for medical aids in case of emergency. WAITER uses three sensors to collect users' vital signals. Bluetooth ear-set is used as a device. WAITER sends health reports to medical centre every one hour.

ANGELAH (Taleb et al. 2009) works well for elders when they are at Home. IMHMS (Shahriyar et al. 2009) gives feedback to user about their health condition but it cannot detect user's location exactly when they are away from home and give immediate treatment in case of emergency. mPHASIS (Kulkarni & Ozturk 2011) wearable sensors will allow to collect vast amount of data and that data can be mined for clinical trials. UHaS (Kang et al. 2011) the wearable devices capture personal vital sign from a user and forward to a PDA and process the data and forwards the data to a health portal.

2.3   RFID

Denis (2016) addresses an important, frequently considered problem in medical settings where a cluster of computationally-weak devices for example RFIDs has to act in an organized manner. Such clusters should act in a way where it can be proved that the responses are obtained simultaneously. A straightforward consequence is a requirement for lightweight cryptographic protocols. Cryptographic protocols design is a tricky issue, also adding stringent computing resources and power limitations results in additional complexity for RFIDs. Knowing further that these devices are becoming rapidly adopted in medical settings, appropriate solutions are of utmost importance (Granjal et al. 2015). Incrementally build protocols based on protocols which have been subject to scientific scrutiny. It makes sense to avoid designing a new solution from scratch to minimize the possibility that the developed solution would turn out to be just another Pandora's Box (Trček & Brodnik 2013). (Abadi & Needham 1996) presented the principles for the design of secure cryptographic protocols. There are two basic principles one is every message should say what it means and its interpretation should be based on only content and other one is the conditions for a message to be acted upon should be clearly set out so that someone reviewing a design may see whether they are acceptable or not.

Yang & Huang (2014) designed Appearance-Based Multimodal Human Tracking and Identification for Healthcare in the Digital Home to track patient around home. (Najera et al. 2011) designed a Real-time location and inpatient care systems based on passive RFID to track patient around hospital's premises. (Juels 2004) introduced the need for proofs of simultaneous presence of RFIDs and coined the term Yoking proofs. These are intended to cover scenarios where proofs of simultaneous scanning of RFIDs are needed.

Juels (2004) work has gained interest in this field and soon research followed that found attacks against it. The first one was done by (Saito & Sakurani 2005) where they proposed timestamps to cure the discovered weakness. However, this improved scheme of Saito and Sakurani was also vulnerable to reply attacks, as discovered by (Piramuthu 2007). If an attacker submits a future timestamp and obtains the response from the first tag it can be later used by the attacker when the corresponding time becomes true. There are many unclear issues with Piramuthu's version. This version gives good grounds to attacks because of not adhering to prudent security protocol engineering principles.

Peris-Lopez et al. (2007) showed (Piramuthu 2007) improvement is claimed to be vulnerable and can be attacked. Also they showed that there is no privacy identifiers of tags A and B are sent in plaintext. So (Peris-Lopez et al. 2007) presented a new scheme called Clumping proof, where they include, explicitly, the verifier in the proof-generating phase. This entity is first mutually authenticated with a reader, and then a timestamp TS is exchanged. This timestamp is encrypted by the verifier.

The Clumping proof scheme does introduce some improvements, one of them being use of counters and chaining of all calculations. But this scheme also needs improvement the hashed timestamp is an inherent point of attack. An attacker can shuffle a bit of the timestamp exchanged at the beginning between the verifier and reader and this cannot be noticed until the verifier checks the proof.

Cho et al. (2008) presented a variant of Piramuthu's protocol. Later, protocols that support anonymization are presented by (Burmester et al. 2008) and (Chien & Liu 2009). Malfunctioning or malicious tags can lead to calculation of useless proofs and denial of service attacks. Therefore on-line authentication schemes should be deployed. (Chien et al. 2010) developed

off-line grouping verification scheme. The reason is on-line grouping proofs
are better replaced by on-line authentication schemes where proofs of
simultaneous reading are formed by trusted back-ends.

Pedro et al. (2010) analyzed all the above discussed protocols for
their weaknesses and computational costs. Author showed that all these
protocols are vulnerable. (Peris-Lopez et al. 2011) proposed a comprehensive
RFID solution to enhance inpatient medication safety. (Safkhani et al. 2014)
showed that (Peris-Lopez et al. 2011) protocol is vulnerable. (Peinado &
Amparo 2014) designed solution suited for Electronic product code
generation 2 tags.

RFID research and development are focusing on manufacturing and
retail sectors to improve supply chain efficiency and learn more about
consumer behavior. After manufacturing and retail industry, Healthcare
domain made attention to the RFID researchers and development team (Fisher
& Monahan 2008). Already some hospitals and medical institutes are starting
to use RFID for patient identification (Xiao et al. 2006), drug administration,
access to medical records, transfusion, and equipment, patient, and staff
tracking. The main purpose of the RFID research is to improve patient's
safety, eliminate paper-based document, cost savings, increases efficiency and
productivity, prevent/reduce medical errors, and so on.

RFID system works by placing unique electronic identifiers on
items or on people. For example, RFIDs can be embedded in patient bracelets
so that medical staffs can do patient identification easily before surgery and
before administering medications and doing blood transfusions. RFID
technology helps in transmitting and receiving data from a patient to medical
professionals without human intervention. Nowadays, most of the hospitals
are focusing on how to improve safety, quality, and value in healthcare. The
application of RFID in healthcare has just begun.

Ayoade (2006) proposed a framework for paperless electronic health record (EHR) system. The authority of readers should be different for accessing different tags. In such cases, proposed RFID access control mechanisms by (Gao et al. 2004), (Chien 2006), (Kim et al. 2006) are not suitable. Also, (Ayoade 2006) did not propose how to make it work in practical.

Chen et al. (2012) have proposed authentication protocols for tamper resistant prescription. Even though server does verification between reader and tag, there is a possibility for mishandling or interchanging tag and reader knowingly or unknowingly. Since only devices are authenticated not the user using these devices. Also, their protocol does not address multiple readers' scenario.

CHAPTER 3

ENERGY EFFICIENT AND LOAD BALANCED WIRELESS SENSOR NETWORK FOR WEARABLE PHYSIOLOGICAL MONITORING

In this chapter importance of wireless sensor network used in wearable physiological monitoring is discussed. Also how energy efficiency can be improved to increase life time of sensor network. Integration of WBAN and WSN are also discussed.

3.1 INTRODUCTION

Traditional healthcare system monitoring setup is not very comfortable and does not provide any freedom to patients. Also, this system cannot be used for wearable physiological monitoring applications because of their large size it could not be wearied (Raskovic et al. 2004). Over a period of time gels used in electrodes can be harmful to skin and can affect signal quality. Hence wearable physiological monitoring systems need to be developed (Pandian et al. 2008).

The wearable physiological monitoring system consists of three systems namely integrated sensors, wearable data acquisition and processing hardware and remote monitoring station. There are number of wearable physiological monitoring systems such as smart vest, AMON, vivometrics, life shirt, life guard and MagIC were developed to monitor the health status of wearer.

The traditional wearable physiological systems has drawbacks such as noise problem, location of sensors cannot be changed, heavy load for processing unit, and cables of sensors can get damaged very easily due to turning of cables. These drawbacks can be solved by wireless sensor networks.

A number of small wireless sensor nodes placed on human body can create a wireless body area network which can monitor vital signals of the wearer and it can send the report to the user and doctor. A network can be formed by deploying sensor nodes in an adhoc manner with no predefined routes.

Physiological monitoring can be done by wireless sensor network which has three modules such as integrated sensor nodes, wearable data acquisition and processing hardware (sink node) and remote monitoring station. Since sensor nodes in wireless sensor network have limited energy that energy should be preserved to maintain network life time. Clustering is an effective technique which is useful in extending life time of wireless sensor network. Low-Energy Adaptive Clustering Hierarchy (LEACH) uses single-hop communication; it cannot be deployed in networks spread over large distances.

LEACH cannot provide actual load balancing. Cluster heads are elected only on the basis of probability, not taking energy into consideration and uniform distribution cannot be ensured. Thus, nodes with lower energy will be selected as cluster heads, which leads to death of these nodes very quickly.

Reselection-based Energy Efficient Routing Algorithm (REERA) is an improvement of LEACH (Wang et al. 2013). In this work REERA has been extended and compared with Energy LEACH (E-LEACH), Weighted

LEACH (W-LEACH), and LEACH implemented using fuzzy logic (LEACH-FL) and Load Balancing among cluster heads using min heap algorithm is discussed.

3.2 LEACH

LEACH is a kind of cluster-based routing protocols, which uses distributed cluster formation. LEACH randomly, selects a few sensor nodes as cluster heads (CHs) and rotates this role to evenly distribute the energy load among the sensors in the network. The idea is to form clusters of the sensor nodes based on the received signal strength and use local cluster heads as routers to the sink. In LEACH, the Cluster Heads compress data arriving from member nodes and send an aggregated packet to the BS.

In order to reduce the amount of information that must be transmitted to the BS. In order to reduce inter & intra cluster interference LEACH uses a TDMA/code-division multiple access (CDMA) MAC.

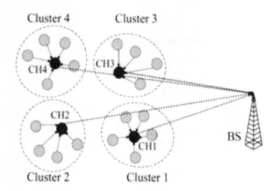

Figure 3.1 LEACH Clustering Hierarchy Model

Figure 3.1 shows LEACH clustering hierarchy and how clusters are formed and communication to base station.

The operation of LEACH is done into two steps, the setup phase and the steady state phase. In setup phase the nodes are organized into clusters and CHs are selected. The node is selected as a cluster head for the current round if the random number is less than the threshold value T (n), which is given by

$$T(n) = \begin{cases} \frac{p}{1-p*(r mod \frac{1}{p})} & if \ n \in G \\ 0 & otherwise \end{cases} \tag{3.1}$$

In the steady state phase, the actual data is transferred to the BS. To minimize overhead the duration of the steady state phase should be longer than the duration of the setup phase. The CH node, after receiving all the data from its member nodes, performs aggregation before sending it to the BS. After a certain time period, the setup phase is restarted and new CHs are selected.

3.3 ENERGY LEACH

Energy-LEACH protocol improves the cluster head selection procedure. It makes residual energy of node as the main matrix which decides whether these nodes turn into cluster head or not in the next round. In first round communication, every node has the same probability to turn into cluster head. Figure 3.2 shows how clusters are formed in E-LEACH.

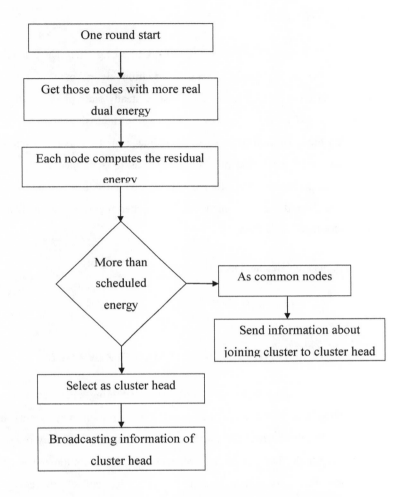

Figure 3.2 Flow Chart of E-LEACH Cluster Formation Phase

3.4   WEIGHTED LEACH

Weighted Low Energy Adaptive Clustering Hierarchy Aggregation (W-LEACH), is a centralized data aggregation algorithm. As in LEACH, W-LEACH consists of a setup phase and a steady state phase. In the setup phase, W-LEACH first calculates a weight value and assigns it to each sensor. Modified the definition of to be the percentage of the maximum number of CHs instead of the actual number of CHs as it is defined in the original LEACH. A maximum of % of alive sensors are then selected to be CHs based on the calculated weights, such that the higher the weights the better the chance for them to be CHs.

The weights are calculated as follows:

$$w_i = \begin{cases} e_i * d_i \ if \ d_i > d_{threshold} \\ d_i \qquad\qquad otherwise \end{cases} \tag{3.2}$$

3.5   LEACH IMPLEMENTED USING FUZZY LOGIC

To achieve high energy efficiency, gathering and calculating other information that could affect the energy consumption may occurs heavy overhead. So, the overhead of cluster head election may be highly reduced by using fuzzy logic. Three fuzzy variables (energy, concentration and centrality) were used for fuzzy if-then rule. The base station collects the energy and location information from all sensor nodes and elects the cluster heads using fuzzy if-then rule according to the collected fuzzy variables.

1.	/*for every round */
2.	if rand() $< p_{opt}$ then
3.	Compute the chance using Fuzzy if-then rule;
4.	AdvCandidate_Message(chance);
5.	myCH=me;
6.	while receiving Candidate-Message from node N
7.	if chance < N's chance then
8.	myCH N;
9.	chance N's chance;
10.	endif
11.	end while
12.	if myCH==me then
13.	AdvCH-Message;
14.	Endif
15.	Else
16.	On receiving CH-message
17.	Select the closest CH;
18.	Send Cluster_Join_Message to the closest CH;
19.	End if

Figure 3.3 Clustering Algorithm using Fuzzy Logic

In Figure 3.3 clustering algorithm used by fuzzy logic was discussed and in Table 3.1 fuzzy if then rule was discussed.

Table 3.1 Fuzzy if then rule

	Energy	**Local distance**	**Chance**
1	Low	Far	Very low
2	Low	Medium	Low
3	Low	Close	Rather low
4	Medium	far	Med low
5	Medium	Medium	Med
6	Medium	close	Med high
7	High	far	Rather high
8	High	Medium	High
9	High	close	Very high

3.6   NETWORK MODEL

A set of sensors are randomly dispersed to continuously monitor the surrounding environment. The entire network is divided into several clusters with different size as shown in network model. In each cluster, there is a cluster head, which can perform data fusion after collecting all the raw data from its ordinary members.

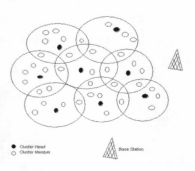

Figure 3.4 Network model

Figure 3.4 shows cluster head, cluster member and base station as a network model.

3.7   ENERGY MODEL

The famous first order radio is used as the energy model. If the distance between the transmitter and the receiver is larger than a threshold d_0, the multi-path (d^4 power loss) model is used; otherwise, the free space (d^2 power loss) is used. Therefore, the energy spent to transmit an l-bit packet over distance d can be calculated as follows (Wang et al. 2013).

$$E_{Tx}(l,d) = \begin{cases} lE_{elec} + 1\varepsilon_{fs}d^2, & d < d_0 \\ lE_{elec} + 1\varepsilon_{mp}d^4, & d \geq d_0 \end{cases} \tag{3.3}$$

Where E_{elec} denotes the electronics energy, which depends on factors such as the digital coding, modulation and so on; ε_{fs} and ε_{mp} denotes the amplifier energy to maintain an acceptable signal-to-noise ratio; d_0=sqrt($\varepsilon_{fs}/\varepsilon_{mp}$) is a constant. The energy spent to receive this message can be calculated as follows:

$$E_{Rx}(l) = lE_{elec} \tag{3.4}$$

3.8   RESELECTION ALGORITHM

Reselection-based Energy Efficient Routing Algorithm consists of three fundamental phases as follows: candidate cluster heads selection phase, cluster formation and final cluster heads selection phase and the data transmission phase (Wang et al. 2013).

68

3.8.1 Cluster Head Selection Phase

The base station broadcasts a BS_ADV message to all the nodes after network deployment at a certain power level. According to the received signal strength each node will compute its approximate distance d to the base station and also computes a parameter K^i which is set as following:

$$K^i = E_{residual} / d(i, BS) \qquad (3.5)$$

Where $E_{residual}$ represents the residual energy of node and d(i,BS) is the distance between node and the base station.

Here, d_{max} and d_{min} represent the maximum distance and the minimum distance between sensor nodes and the base station. The competition radius R^i of the node is computed by the following equation:

$$R^i = \frac{(d_{max} - d_{min})*d(i,BS)}{d_{max}} + d_{min} \qquad (3.6)$$

Probability T(n) value helps each node to decide whether they can be able to compete to be a cluster head. Nodes are deployed randomly and when no of nodes are larger than the threshold value then the node becomes a member node. Otherwise, it can be within the cluster radius of other candidate cluster heads. If it is true, the node releases it from the competition and becomes a member node. If it is not true, then the nodes select it to be a cluster head and inform all the neighbor nodes through messages.

3.8.2 Cluster Formation and Final Cluster Heads Selection Phase

According to the received signal strength all cluster members finds to which cluster they can be associated. After finding the cluster head they inform that they wish to join as a member by sending a JOIN_MSG (ID,K^i).

ANNA UNIVERSITY, CHENNAI - 600 025

After receiving all the JOIN_MSG from its own cluster members cluster head finds member node which has the large K value. The cluster head die early due to transmission distance and heavy traffic. So to save energy consumption in the entire network, nodes close to the base station and which has more residual energy can be selected as cluster heads.

According the value of K, the final cluster heads is selected. All nodes and previous cluster head in each cluster sends a message which contains the ID to the node which has the biggest value of K and becomes member of this node. The final cluster head is the node which receives all these messages and creates a TDMA schedule, according to the schedule it informs their member nodes to forward the data which is sensed by them.

3.8.3   Data Transmission Phase

After the final cluster heads selection and the TDMA schedules are decided then data transmission can be started. According to the TDMA schedule member nodes belongs to their cluster head will send their sensed data based on their slot allocated to them.

In order to save energy consumption all node radio signal will be turned on only when their allocated slot comes. The cluster heads by using multi-hop transmission sends data to the base station after doing data fusion. Data fusion is done after receiving all the data from their member nodes. Like this next round begins over a period of time which is predefined.

3.9   LOAD BALANCING USING MIN HEAP ALGORITHM

Clustering mechanism can be used for load balancing. Cluster–Head is responsible for the creating cluster and performance of cluster is affected by cluster nodes (Kuilab & Jana 2012).

A min binary heap is a complete binary tree which has keys and objects stored at the nodes, such that a node's key is greater than or equal to its parent's nodes. Heap is described as smallest ones will be at the top.

Cluster head which is at root from the min-heap is picked which has the minimum number of sensor nodes allotted to it and assign a sensor node to that Cluster head. Therefore, the cluster heads which is minimum loaded is distributed with the available loads; thereby load balancing among Cluster heads is shown in the figure 3.5 distance between two nodes decides energy consumption.

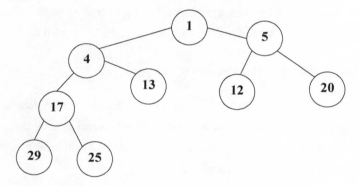

Figure 3.5 Min Heap Tree

Figure 3.5 shows how min heap tree is constructed and minimum number will be at the root. By assigning the sensor node to nearest minimum loaded Cluster head in their assignment round. Energy consumption of all sensor nodes has been reduced. Thus the min heap algorithm considers load balancing of the Cluster heads and the energy efficiency of the sensor nodes.

Types of Sensor Nodes:

Depending on the communication range between the sensor nodes and the gateways, there can be two kinds "restricted node" and "open node".

- Restricted Node: Restricted nodes are those sensor nodes, which can communicate with one and only one gateway.

- Restricted Set: Restricted set is the set of all restricted nodes in the WSN. We refer this set as "R_{set}". It is obvious to note that sensor S$_i$ belongs to R_{set} if it is satisfies the following criteria:

$$S_i \in R_{set} \left[\{G_j \in Com(S_i) | G_j \in \zeta\} \wedge \{G_k \notin Com(S_i) | \forall G_k \in (\zeta - G_j)\} \right] \quad (3.7)$$

Where, Com (S_i) is the set of all those gateways, which are within communication range of S_i and ζ is the set of all gateways.

- Open Node: Open nodes are those sensor nodes, which can communicate with more than one gateway.

- Open Set: Open set is a collection of all open nodes in the WSN. We refer this set as "O_{set}". A sensor node S_l is belongs to O_{set}, if it satisfies the following criteria:

$$S_i \in O_{set} \Leftrightarrow [S_i \notin R_{set}] \quad (3.8)$$

Minheap algorithm

Input:

A set of sensors T = $\{S_1, S_2, \ldots \ldots S_n\}$

A set of cluster heads $\zeta = \{G_1, G_2, \ldots \ldots G_n\}$ where m<n

$d_{ij} = \forall S_i, G_j$, the distance between S_i to G_j; where $G_j \in Com(S_i)$

R_{set} and O_{set}

Output:

An assignment A:T → ζ such that the overall maximum number of sensor node of CHs and total consumed energy is minimized.

Step 1:   While($R_{set} \neq NULL$)

{

Assign successive sensor nodes S_i to their corresponding gateway G_j such that

$S_i \in R_{set}$ and $G_j \in Com(S_i)$ and delete S_i from R_{set} and T

}

Step 2:   Build a min-heap using the gateways on the number of allotted sensor nodes to the gateways

Step 3:   While (T≠ $NULL$)

{

Step 3.1:   Pick up the root node of the min-heap say G_j

Step 3.2:   Select and assign a sensor (Open) node S_i to G_j such that $G_j \in Com(S_i)$ and S_i is nearest sensor node to G_j

Step 3.3:   Delete S_i from T

Step 3.4:   Adjust the min-heap so that the minimum loaded gateway will be at root

}

Step 4:   Stop

Time complexity of algorithm is O log(N).

3.10   SIMULATION PARAMETERS AND RESULTS

MATLAB is used to evaluate the performance of the algorithms discussed above. Assumptions are made by creating 100 sensor nodes with the same initial energy which are distributed randomly in a square region of $100 \times 100 \text{ m}^2$ and relevant simulation parameters are listed in Table 3.2.

Table 3.2 Simulation Parameters

Parameters	Definition	Unit
N	Number of sensor nodes	100
E_0	Initial energy of sensor nodes	2J
R	Transmission radius	50m
E_{elec}	Energy dissipation to run the radio device	50nJ/bit
ε_{fs}	Free space model of transmitter amplifier	10pJ/bit/m2
ε_{mp}	Multi-path model of transmitter amplifier	0.0013pJ/bit/m4
L	Packet length	2000 bits
d_0	Distance threshold	$\sqrt{\dfrac{\varepsilon_{fs}}{\varepsilon_{mp}}}$
BS_Location	Base station position	(200,50)

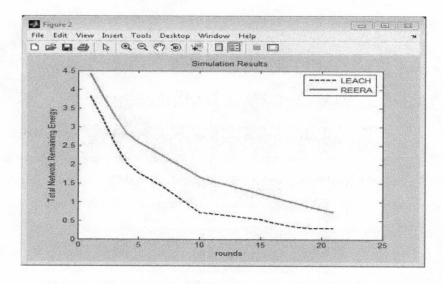

Figure 3.6 Network Lifetime Comparisons of REERA and LEACH

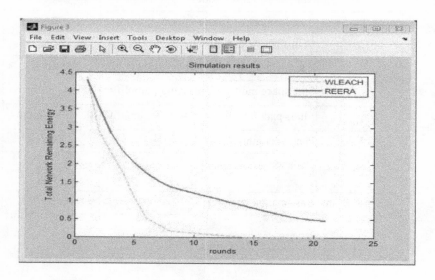

Figure 3.7 Network Lifetime Comparisons of REERA and WLEACH

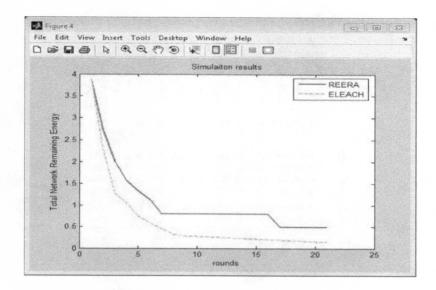

Figure 3.8 Network Lifetime Comparisons of REERA and ELEACH

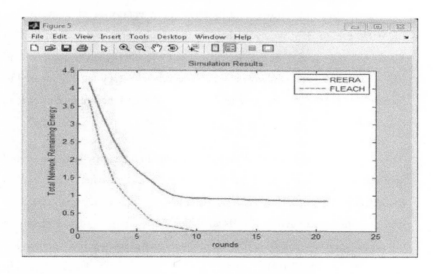

Figure 3.9 Network Lifetime Comparisons of REERA and FLEACH

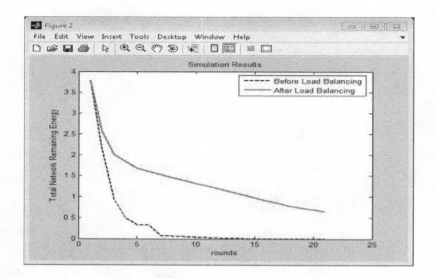

Figure 3.10 Load Balancing in REERA

Figure 3.6 shows REERA has more energy level compared to LEACH, Figure 3.7 Shows REERA has more energy level compared to WLEACH, Figure 3.8 Shows REERA has more energy level compared to ELEACH and Figure 3.9 Shows REERA has more energy level compared to FLEACH. Figure 3.10 Shows energy level of REERA before and after load balancing.

In Figure 3.8 and Figure 3.9 the network remaining energy is stable from 7 approximately because total energy used by REERA when compared to ELEACH and FLEACH is very less. Reselection of cluster head based on energy leads to number of rounds in which node energy lost completely is minimized. In REERA from 7 approximately nodes energy level draining is stable whereas in ELEACH and FLEACH node energy level is quickly drained.

3.11 WBANs AND WSNs APPLICATION INTEGRATION APPROACH

Worldwide aging of population is a very serious problem. By 2025 people over 65 years old will reach 761 million (Weiya & Chao 2009). Also, according to Department of Health of China, illness people above 65 years are 3.2 times of other population and health resources cost compared to others is 1.9 times more. These data shows that the current health care systems are facing challenges. Also, in Pakistan in the year 2007-2008 total health care expenditure was Rs. 3.791 billion and expected to increase in the coming years (Sandhu et al. 2014).

Health care cost can be reduced by monitoring patient vital signs remotely and continuously. For patient, soldiers and athletes monitoring of human body and surrounding environment is important.

A subclass of WSN called WBAN consists of small-sized, low power and intelligent nodes. Sensors used in WBAN are on-body and in-body which can be placed on human body for health monitoring. WBAN provides very good health monitoring for human without affecting their routine activities. WBAN and WSN application integrated approach can be used for continuous healthcare monitoring. Patient or solider fatigue can also be monitored by using this application.

By integrating both WBAN and WSN quality of life can be improved. Also, both WBAN and WSN nodes have very limited energy. There is no provision to recharge the batteries. Therefore, energy plays vital role in these applications so there is need for energy efficient routing protocol. Sensors used in WBAN and WSN sense and gather data constantly and transmit only on the allocated time slot and based on the residual energy and distance from the base station cluster head is selected. Normally, node with more energy is selected as cluster head.

Clustering technique is used to save energy. Time and Energy aware routing protocol instructs nodes to transmit their data to cluster head or PDA on time slot according to Time Division Multiple Access schedule. Rest of the time nodes just sense the data and keep the data. When it allotted time starts sends the data to the cluster head or PDA. After transmission is over nodes goes to listening mode. In listening mode nodes just does sensing only so energy is saved. Also, when the current cluster head energy is low and new cluster is reselected based on nodes residual energy and distance from the base station. After transmitting data cluster head energy will be drained. So new cluster head selection is necessary. Mobile sink is used to collect data from WSN cluster head and WBAN user. Hence energy is saved in better way.

3.12   PROPOSED PROTOCOL AND HEALTHCARE MODEL

In this work Time and Energy Aware Routing Protocol (TEA) and healthcare model is proposed. Sensors used in WBAN and WSN sense and gather data constantly and transmit only on the allocated time slot and based on residual energy and distance from the base station cluster head is selected. Normally, node with more energy is selected as cluster head. Clustering technique is used to save energy. This protocol instructs nodes to transmit their data to cluster head or Personal Digital Assistant (PDA) on time slot according to Time Division Multiple Access schedule. Rest of the time nodes just sense the data and keep the data. When the allotted time is started this protocol sends the data to the cluster head or PDA. After transmission is over nodes enter in to listening mode. In listening mode nodes just does sensing only so energy is saved.

Also, when the current cluster head energy is low and new cluster is reselected based on nodes residual energy and distance from the base station. After transmitting data cluster head energy will be drained. So new cluster head selection is necessary. Mobile sink is used to collect data from cluster head and WBAN user. Hence energy is saved in better way.

Figure 3.11 shows the proposed healthcare model. First wireless body area networks sensors are integrated and their batteries can be powered by human body heat, walking, solar panel circuit integrated in it and near-field communication. WBAN sensed data can be sent to PDA and wireless sensor network region cluster head. Second wireless sensor networks nodes batteries are powered by solar panel and near-field communication. Mobile sink collects data from the region cluster head and transmits to base station. Third from the base station data is transmitted to remote healthcare center or hospitals through WiFi or internet. By this way this model helps to save energy efficiently and quality of life is improved in a better way.

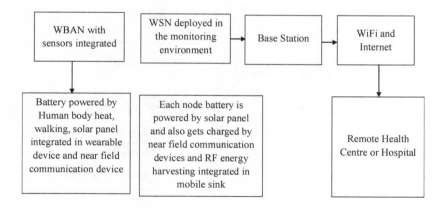

Figure 3.11 Proposed Healthcare Model

3.13   SIMULATION AND RESULTS

NS2 is used for simulation purpose and simulation parameters are given in Table 3.3. Totally 13 nodes have been deployed. After deployment of nodes based on their residual energy cluster head has been selected and it is divided as region1 and region2. Region1 has node0, node1, node2, node3, and node4. Node1 becomes cluster head in region1. Similarly region2 has node5, node6, node7, node8, node9. Node5 becomes cluster head in region2. Node10 is assumed to be base station, node11 is mobile sink and node12 is user who is wearing WBAN devices with PDA having Bluetooth.

Table 3.3 Simulation and Results

Parameters	Values
Protocol	DSDV
Simulation environment	NS2
Simulation time	205sec
Simulation area	881X652m
Nodes used	13
Mobility model	Fixed way point
Traffic type	CBR
CBR data rate	5, 10, 15, 20 packets/sec
Packet size	512 bytes
Transmission range	250m
Link capacity	2Mbps
MAC	802.11

Figure 3.12 shows the initial deployment of sensor nodes. Figure 3.13 shows the base station, mobile sink (node10 which is red in color

is assumed to be the base station and node11 which is blue in color is assumed to be the mobile sink) and user wearing WBAN devices (node12 which is violet in color is assumed to be the WBAN user). Figure 3.14 shows region1 cluster head (green color) and region2 cluster head (green color) selection. Figure 3.15 shows data transmission among region1 nodes (yellow color) to cluster head. Figure 3.16 shows movement of WBAN node in to region1, movement of mobile sink to region1 and data transfer between region1 cluster head and mobile sink. Figure 3.17 shows data transmission among WBAN node to region1 cluster head. Figure 3.18 shows data transmission among mobile sink to the base station. Similarly region2 also does data transmission as region1. Figure 3.19 shows region2 node data transfer to cluster head of region2. Figure 3.20 shows WBAN node data transfer to the cluster head of region2 when it is moving in region2. Figure 3.21 shows data transfer among region2 cluster head and mobile sink. Figure 3.22 shows data transfer among mobile sink and base station.

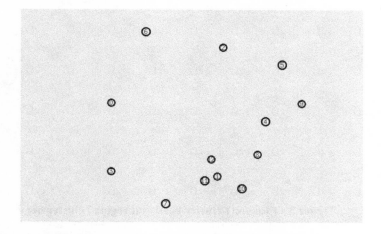

Figure 3.12 Initial deployment of sensor nodes

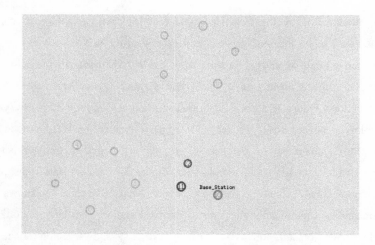

Figure 3.13 Base station, mobile sink and WBAN user

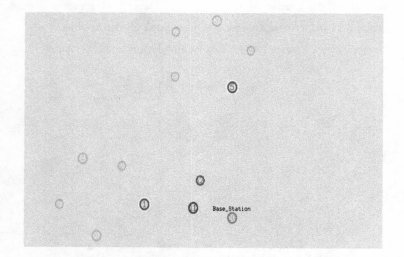

Figure 3.14 Region1 cluster head and region2 cluster head

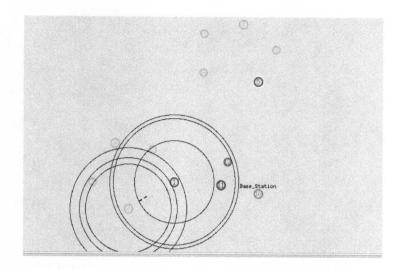

Figure 3.15 Data transmission among region1 nodes to cluster head

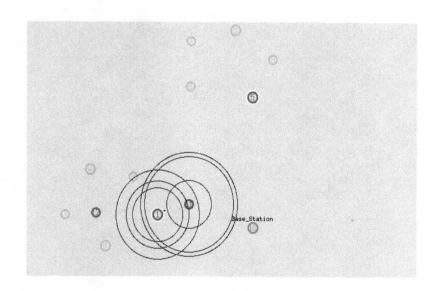

Figure 3.16 Movement of WBAN node

84

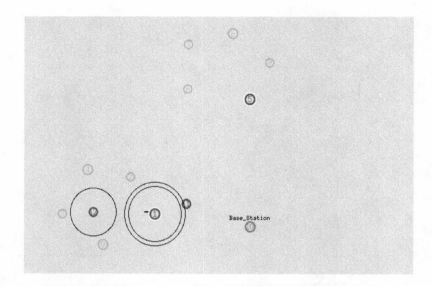

Figure 3.17 Data transmission among WBAN node to region1 cluster head

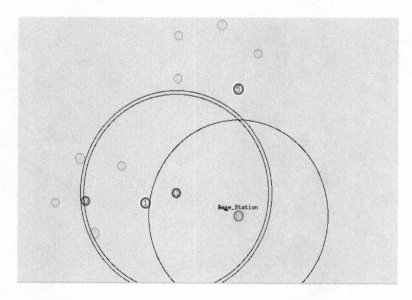

Figure 3.18 Data transmission among mobile sink to the base station

 ANNA UNIVERSITY, CHENNAI - 600 025

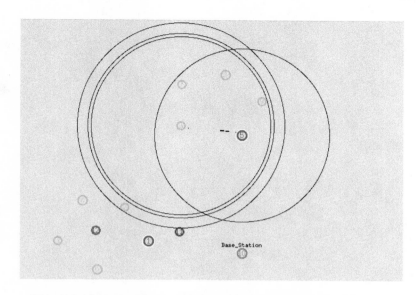

Figure 3.19 Region2 node data transfer to cluster head of region2

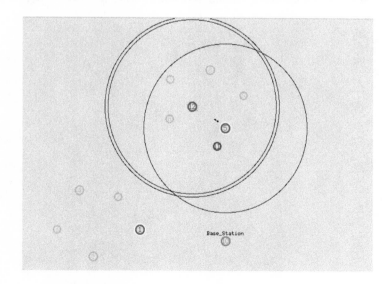

Figure 3.20 WBAN node data transfer to the cluster head of region2 when it is moving in region2

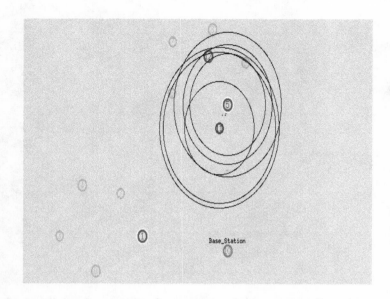

Figure 3.21 Data transfer among region2 cluster head and mobile sink

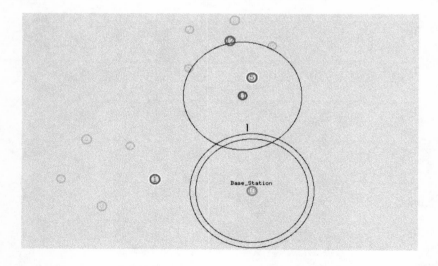

Figure 3.22 Data transfer among mobile sink and base station

Thus, these simulation results shows that data transferred is at fixed time and cluster head will be collecting data from its members as well as from WBAN users at fixed time. By making all the nodes after data transfer to listening mode energy can be saved. In listening mode all nodes will be doing sensing activity only. Mobile sink node has more energy compared to all nodes. Hence energy is saved more by this time and energy aware protocol (TEA).

3.14 CONCLUSION

A wearable wireless sensor network of physiological integrated sensors placed in user collects data and transmits continuously to a remote monitoring station where the user health status is remotely monitored. The wearable physiological monitoring systems should provide accurate data recordings compared to traditional monitoring systems. The devices used should have time stamped data storage without any failures it should do continuous monitoring. Monitoring continuously will help to detect disease earlier and increase the level of confidence among patients and in turn it can improve quality life of user. This allows user to do their daily activities without any problem. There is no need for the user to stay at home. Users are free to move around without any problem.

One of the most problem in wireless sensor network is energy on network nodes is very limited. Hence, energy efficient is needed for increasing network lifetime. The maximum energy is lost by data transmission and communication. Clustering helps to solve this problem. Leach is one of clustering mechanisms which can help in prolonging the network lifetime. Reselection based energy efficient routing algorithm discussed in this paper can improve better than LEACH. Hence, simulation results show that this Reselection technique is better in energy efficient compared with WLEACH, ELEACH and LEACH-FL. Also, by using min heap algorithm load balancing among cluster heads is done to improve energy efficiency.

Future work is to reduce Noise in data recordings of WBAN and WSN and to implement Expected Transmission Count (ETX).

Energy is very important for WBAN and WSN applications. Hence energy saving of sensor node is very challenging for these applications because of very tiny sensors with limited energy in built are used in these applications. In this work, possibilities of achieving energy efficiency and quality of life in healthcare by using the proposed protocol and model are discussed. By integrated approach of WBANs and WSNs how energy can be saved is discussed. Future work is to implement this protocol and model in a real time setup.

CHAPTER 4

EMERGENCY ALERT AND TRACKING SYSTEM FOR WEARABLE PERSONAL HEALTHCARE

In this chapter a novel wearable personal healthcare and emergency alert and tracking system, namely WHEATS is proposed, which can continuously monitor user body status in a real-time manner and automatically issue the alert for medical aids in case of emergency is discussed.

4.1   INTRODUCTION

Traditional healthcare system is unable to provide freedom and comfort to patients because of the lack of monitoring setup. Growth of wireless communication helps to achieve dynamic monitoring setup in today and future healthcare systems and it also reduces the patients' discomfort like staying long in hospitals, home, etc. It also reduces maintenance cost and aids to achieve pervasive and mobile health care. Healthcare professionals can use pervasive and mobile computing, wearable biosensors and wireless communication technologies to perform early diagnosis and treatment, and develop and verify new therapies through continuously monitoring and analyzing human vital signs. Humans can be tracked and monitored using wearable and non-wearable sensor devices (Ameen & Kwak 2011).

Body sensor network(BSN), also known as body area sensor network(BASN), is a sensor network whose nodes are biosensors either implanted in, worn on, or close to human bodies. BSN helps to achieve pervasive and mobile healthcare features completely. The role of body sensor networks in healthcare is to minimize the need for caregivers and help the people to live independently and provides quality care (Darwish & Hassanien 2011) .

A BSN usually consists of implantable or wearable biosensors, such as pulse oximetry, glucose sensor, ECG, phonocardiography (PCG), ambulatory blood pressure (ABP) and oxygen saturation (SPO2) sensors, piezoplethysmography or photoplethysmography (PPG) ring sensor, temperature sensor, and even ingestible camera pills. These sensors are capable of monitoring vital signs continuously and reporting data to a powerful external device, such as a laptop, personal digital assistant (PDA), a cell phone, or a wrist-worn smart watch (Li & Tan 2010). Raw sensor data or patient events and context can be transmitted to mobile phones or servers for storage or streamed to medical personnel for real-time monitoring of the patient condition. Patients' electronic medical record (EMR) can be processed from WIM embedded in SIM card which provides security while sending health data to hospital server (Ku et al. 2006).

WIM can also be used to enter in to nearby networked healthcare centre. EMR can be sent via GSM module, GPRS, SMS (Short Messaging Service), MMS (Multimedia Messaging Service), and Wi-fi (Wireless fidelity) connection sickness prevention and early diagnosis saves lives.

Bluetooth–enabled devices have also been successfully tested in the hospital environment (Wu et al. 2008). The Bluetooth wireless communication device includes microprocessor and Bluetooth wireless transceiver for data communication. This device provides a wireless channel between the wearable vital signal collection devices and the mobile phone.

Development of mobile and pervasive computing technologies can provide better personal healthcare in a low cost manner compared to traditional technologies. However, the implementation of a feasible personal healthcare and emergency alert and tracking system is not easy due to the following challenging issues:

- All the health care center system should be networked to a centralized health care center system.

- The need for integrating different sensors into one solution makes it harder as in the sensor units of LiveNet (Sung et al. 2005) and PATHS (Li & Zhang 2007).

- Users' privacy violation policy and social issues should not be overlooked.

- Designing wearable vital sensors should consider the user comfort and it should not affect the user's behaviors.

- Data collected from sensors need on-site processing, filtering, mining and storing. It is widely accepted that the wireless data transmission costs very high energy consumption. The on-site data processing and filtering, mining and storing can significantly reduce the amount of raw data to reduce the energy consumption in data transmission.

- The collected data should be periodically sent to centralized healthcare centre.

- Healthcare centre allow medical experts to monitor the health status of users.

- The system should detect the emergency and send the alert to the nearby healthcare centre for timely medical aid.

First, this system does not need any specific care givers and is easily used. Second, WHEATS employs the ECG, blood pressure, body temperature, motion, blood oxygen saturation (SPO2) and glucose sensors to continuously collect users' vital signals. Also, we use tiny Bluetooth device to transmit the raw sensory data. From the users' point of view, the device attached on the body is just a Bluetooth wrist watch device. This system does not affect their daily activities and it is not inconvenience to their life. Wrist-watch device can also be used for fall detection (Holzinger et al. 2010).

Third, we use a mobile phone equipped with Bluetooth transceiver to receive sensory data from Bluetooth device (which collects sensor data from all sensors), to perform on-site data processing and storage, which avoids the continuous connection to the healthcare centre and reduces transmission cost. The mobile phone can use the attached GSM module, GPRS, SMS, Wi-Fi and MMS to periodically send the health reports to the medical centre and issue timely alerts for medical aid in case of emergency. In case of emergency, ECG, blood pressure and other required vital signs and EMR are sent through MMS and SMS to the healthcare centre system via nearby hospital care centre system and also to Doctors' mobile/PC (Sufi et al. 2009).

WIM helps mobile phone to send secure patient data. By receiving data, Doctor can treat patient by seeing EMR and analyze the data for prevention of disease. Thus, patient life is saved.

Patient exact location is tracked by A-GPS and intimated to the ambulance for rescuing the patient from the danger by providing appropriate treatment. In case of emergency, mobile phone dials four numbers such as family members, friends, neighbors and ambulance number. Audio messaging can also be done. WHEATS can satisfy the requirements of personal healthcare and emergency alert and tracking system in an effective, simple and low-cost manner.

4.2   PROPOSED SYSTEM FEATURES

The proposed system WHEATS has following features compared to the existing system:

- WHEATS is not restricted to any space and the user is allowed freely to go wherever they wish.

- WHEATS can collect the health status data of users and transmit them to the healthcare centre, which can be very helpful to the sickness prevention and early diagnosis.

- WHEATS allows the caregivers to more accurately understand the status of the patient based on the collected sensory data rather than the patient own oral description. In addition, WHEATS can automatically ask for the emergency aid even when the users are unconscious.

- WHEATS just uses Bluetooth to combine the wearable data collection device and mobile phone, which is cost effective and more convenient to use for the user.

- WHEATS uses ECG, blood pressure, body temperature, motion, blood oxygen saturation (SPO2) and glucose sensors.

- WHEATS sends data every half an hour to healthcare centre because it is necessary for analyzing and diagnoses health condition.

- WHEATS uses WIM for secure data transfer to healthcare centre because patient health data is sensitive. WHEATS sends data first to nearby healthcare centre and then to centralized healthcare centre server. By this way patient gets early treatment compared to existing systems.

- WHEATS uses A-GPS to track user location exactly and SMS, MMS, and GPRS for data transmission.

- WHEATS uses Wrist watch device which is useful and comfortable to the user.

- WHEATS communicates to four numbers in case of emergency. Audio messaging is also possible. Based on the motion information, fall detection is possible.

- npowerPEG (Personal Energy Generator) (Cephik et al. 2013) is used in WHEATS for mobile phone charging when the user is moving mobile phone is charged.

- Components used in the system can be powered by solar batteries and human body heat (Leonov & Vullers 2009) and human body motion (Paradiso & Starner 2005).

4.3 COMPARISON OF PROPOSED MODEL WITH EXISTING MODEL

The proposed model is compared with various existing model and their results are shown in table 4.1. The criteria used for comparison are functions covered by the models, cost wise, WIM support wise, Energy management, coverage area and sickness prevention and early diagnosis of the model.

Table 4.1 Comparison of proposed model WHEATS with previous model

Model	Functions covered	WIM support	Cost high or low	Energy management	Coverage area	Sickness prevention and early diagnosis
Elitecare	Personal healthcare	No	high	Bad	Smart space only	Good
CodeBlue	Emergency medical care only	No	high	Bad	Indoor only	No
PEL	Emergency medical care only	No	High	Bad	Indoor only	No
AMON	Continuous monitoring and emergency alert	No	High	Bad	Indoor and outdoor	No
WAITER	Continuous monitoring and emergency alert	No	High	Bad	Indoor and outdoor	Good
ANGELAH	Elders care at Home	No	High	Bad	Indoor only	No
IMHMS	Home only	No	High	Bad	Indoor only	No
Mphasis	Datamining clinical trials	No	High	Bad	Indoor only	No
WHEATS	Continuous monitoring and emergency alert, dials four numbers, track user location	Yes	Low	Very Good	Both indoor and outdoor	Very Good

Proposed model WHEATS uses WIM. By using WIM features such as Security, Digital signature, Authenticate client and server, Mobility, Non-repudiation for e-document transactions, Integrity, Tamper-resistant component, Cryptographic features, Logistics, Portability and Secure sessions can be achieved better (Ku et al. 2006).

Till date no existing models have used WIM. WIM features discussed above makes this model better in cost, security, performance, safe and reliability compared to existing models. Since WIM is a tamper-resistant component important details like patient name, date-of-birth, medical history, and allergy details can be stored which will be very useful in case of emergency.

WHEATS has continuous battery back-up for wearable sensor device by means of integrating solar batteries, human body heat and human body motion. For mobile phone battery back-up npowerPEG can be used. Since battery back-up is important for continuous collection of user's vital signals and for processing vital signals data.

WHEATS automatically dial family members, friends, neighbor and ambulance number in case of emergency. Early diagnosis and disease prevention and medical decision can also be done effectively by using this proposed system. Hence this proposed model WHEATS as a proof-of-concept is best compared to the existing models.

4.4   ARCHITECTURE OF WEARABLE VITAL SIGNAL

Figure 4.1 shows the wearable vital signal collection device which mainly includes six different kinds of vital signal sensors and a Bluetooth wireless communication device. The sensors are ECG, blood pressure, body temperature, motion, blood oxygen saturation (SPO2) and glucose respectively. The ECG sensor is used to record heart beat rate. By recording heart beat rate early diagnosis of heart related problems is possible. Blood pressure sensor is used to record blood pressure reading. High blood pressure and low blood pressure related problems are analyzed. By measuring and monitoring the body movement of the user, motion sensor can help to determine where a user has faced difficulty in movement or fallen at home or road. Hence, instant aid can be given to the user.

Furthermore, the motion information or body movement intensity can act as a reference signal to determine whether the measured signals from other sensors have been affected by the motion of users and be used to minimize the impact of motion to other vital signals (Colin et al. 2004). Blood oxygen saturation is used to record oxygen present in blood. Glucose sensor is used to collect glucose levels in blood and it is used to record blood sugar levels which can be used to detect diabetes related problems.

The Bluetooth wireless communication device includes microprocessor and a Bluetooth wireless transceiver for data communication. This device provides a wireless channel between the wearable vital signal collection devices and the mobile phone. Once the device receives the data from the sensors, it will forward the data immediately to Bluetooth wrist watch device from Bluetooth wrist watch device to the mobile phone via an established Bluetooth data transfer channel. Figure 4.2 shows Bluetooth wrist watch device.

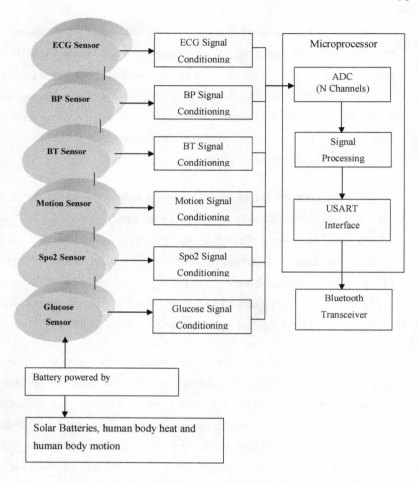

Figure 4.1 Architecture of Wearable vital signal

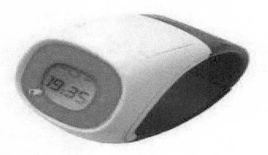

Figure 4.2 Bluetooth wrist watch

This prototype system use a Nokia E500 (Figure 4.3) as on-site data processing and storage centre. It is connected to npowerPEG (Figure 4.4) for charging when user walks or moves in a vehicle. Since Nokia E500 has already been equipped with a Bluetooth transceiver, it can directly receive the raw data sent by wearable vital signal device. Meanwhile, Nokia E500 also supports J2ME and based on the java platform, software is developed to allow the mobile phone to conduct on-site data filtering and validation, 30 minutes report generation, emergency detection, location detection and the alert issuing.

WIM embedded in SIM card gives security for users' health data. After the data processing, the mobile phone can transmit the data to the data server deployed at the nearest local healthcare centre via GSM system, GPRS, Internet, MMS, and SMS then to main healthcare centre. In case of emergency, mobile phone automatically dials to family members, neighbors, friends and ambulance number for immediate help.

Figure 4.3 Nokia E500 Mobile phone

Figure 4.4 npowerPEG

The data server at the healthcare centre is equipped with a GSM module and GPRS. Thus, the server can receive the data reports from the mobile phone for different users. The server will store the reports in the local database and send them to main healthcare centre server. Caregivers can access the database to learn about the users' health status. Also, the server can receive emergency alert from a specific user and then, immediately ask medical aid for the user.

The data server located at the healthcare centre mainly has the four functions 1) receiving the users' half an hour reports from the users' and storing them in the back-end database and gives feedback to user 2) authorizing login request of the caregivers 3) allowing authorized users' accessing the data 4) asking for the medical aid of suitable caregivers. It also calls emergency services when received emergency alert from mobile.

4.5 SYSTEM DESIGN

As shown in Figure 4.5. WHEATS is mainly composed of four components, the wearable vital signal collection devices, the mobile phone, and the server deployed at the healthcare centre. The sensors in the wearable vital signal collection devices will continuously perform a sampling every 0.05 second.

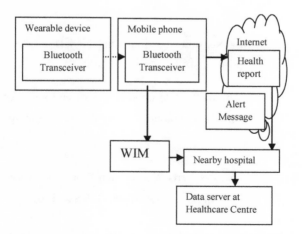

Figure 4.5 System architecture of WHEATS

Also, the Bluetooth transceiver will continuously transmit the raw sensory data to the mobile phone (Figure 4.6).

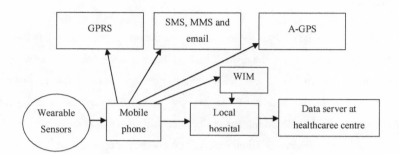

Figure 4.6 Functionalities of the WHEATS system

GPRS- EMR and Health report is sent through GPRS

SMS,MMS and email- Alert is sent to Doctor mobile phone/pc

A-GPS- Tracks user location

WIM- Secure data

Wearable Sensors- Sending vital signals to mobile phone via Bluetooth channel

Mobile phone- Mobile phone receives and analyzes vital signals and produce Half an hour Report and detect Emergency and calls four numbers

Local hospital-alerts doctors and Emergency services and sends data to data server through WIM, GPRS ,Wi-Fi

Data server at healthcare centre- stores all vital signals data gives feedback

The mobile phone can locally process and store the received sensory data. Based on these data, the mobile phone can generate half an hour reports for the users' health status. Also, the mobile phone can detect the emergency of the users and generate an alert for medical aid. Once the mobile phone generates a report or an alert, it uses its GSM module, GPRS, MMS, Wi-Fi and SMS to communicate with the data server at the healthcare centre via local hospital server and transmits the corresponding content to the server as shown in Figure 4.6. In addition, the mobile phone provides interfaces for the users to check and learn about their own health status.

4.6 EVALUATION

To evaluate WHEATS, we have used the following approaches:

1. Implement a prototype of different components of WHEATS.

2. Cognitive walkthrough strategy (Rieman & Redmiles 1995).

4.6.1 Prototype Implementation

Work on building Wearable Body Sensor Network (WBSN) where different sensors are placed in one device is the focus of this work. This implementation is not yet completed fully. So we consider the data provided by the bio-sensors as a well structured XML file.

A sample XML file is shown in Figure 4.7 where a patient's blood pressure, body temperature, blood oxygen saturation (SPO2) and glucose respectively are measured continuously over a period of time. If any of the vital signs is abnormal, then patient data is sent to doctor, family friends, neighbors and healthcare server. WHEATS can be implemented in personal mobile phone. While implementing for Mobile phone, the most suitable communication media between Wearable device and Mobile phone is Bluetooth because of its availability and low cost.

```
<? Xml version= "1.0" encoding="utf-8"?>
<Medical>
<Data>
<Patientname>Archie Stoddart
</Patientname>
<Age>34 </Age>
<SPO2>98(NR: 90-99) </SPO2>
<Temperature> 97 (NR: 98.6)
</Temperature>
<Sugarlevel>110 (NR: 70-100)
</Sugarlevel>
<BP> 98-140 (NR: 120-80) </BP>
</Data>
</Medical>
```

Figure 4.7 Patient's Health Data

For mobile device based implementation J2ME is used. J2ME based custom application can be deployed immediately in a large number of available cell phones or PDA available in the market. The J2ME based mobile phone automatically collects patient's data from the Wearable devices and transfers it to the server and doctor mobile if the data is abnormal. The application can be connected to the server using GPRS, Wi-fi or EDGE. It can connect using SMS if SMS receiving capable application can be developed in the server. The SMS based portion of sending patient data automatically when abnormal vital signals encountered to doctor mobile is implemented.

WBSN collects patient data and send the data to the mobile phone. Mobile phone J2ME application receives the data and process data. Processed data is used to reduce the transmission of unnecessary data to the health centre server.

The Mobile phone communicates with the health centre server nearby using WIM embedded in SIM card and also it can use GPRS, Wi-fi, SMS, MMS and internet. Moreover, the patient's can login to the health centre server using authorized patient-id and password to provide information manually and to view the patient's entire history.

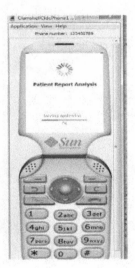

Figure 4.8 Screen shots of patient list

 ANNA UNIVERSITY, CHENNAI - 600 025

Figure 4.9 Patient data

Figure 4.10 SMS sending

Figure 4.11 Received patient data

Some screenshots of these activities are shown in the Figure 4.8 and 4.9. Figure 4.10 shows SMS sending to mobile phone and Figure 4.11 shows received patient data.

Any people with little or no technical knowledge can use it without any difficulties. The communication architecture of WHEATS is very simple and flexible as we claimed. There is no complexity in communication between the components of WHEATS. The prototype implementation requires a cell phone, Bluetooth wrist watch and a WBSN. So the setup for the evaluation is really cost effective.

4.6.2   Cognitive Walkthrough Strategy

Cognitive Walkthrough Strategy encompasses one or a group of evaluators who inspect a user interface by going through a set of tasks and assess its understandability and ease of learning (Polson et al. 1992).

To evaluate WHEATS, strategy followed is: 1. who will be the users of the system? 2 Ph.D. students (Computer Science.), 4 post graduate students (Computer Science.), 2 patients with some technical knowledge and 2 patients without technical knowledge were chosen as the users. We have tried to cover all type of end users and both males and females having different ages. 2. What tasks will be analyzed? The services provided by our WHEATS were executed by the users. We have tried to select the tasks to be analyzed in such a way that no major task has been overlooked. 3. What is the correct action sequence for each task? First, we briefly explained the task sequences and process to get result.

A questionnaire (Table 4.2) was given to the users and discussed the feasibility of the proposed model. The following Figure 4.12 shows the user's satisfaction rating [0 is the lowest value and 5 is the highest value].

Figure 4.12 shows easy to use, satisfaction of service and overall rating of usability issues by users

Rate the proposed model based on the discussion we made: 0 is the lowest value and 5 is the highest value

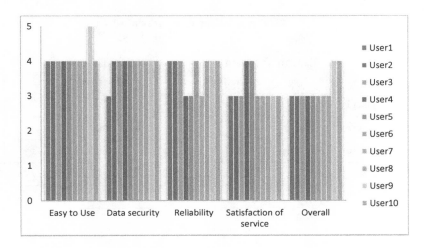

Figure 4.12 Rating of usability issues by users

Table 4.2 WHEATS Questionnaire

Topic	0	1	2	3	4	5
Easy to Use						
Data security						
Reliability						
Satisfaction of Service						
Overall						

Signature of the user

Table 4.3 shows user response to questionnaire and to maintain the privacy of the user details, users are named as 1,2,3,etc.

Table 4.3 User response data

Sl. No	Easy to Use	Data security	Reliability	Satisfaction of service	Overall
User1	4	3	4	3	3
User2	4	4	4	3	3
User3	4	4	4	3	3
User4	4	4	3	4	3
User5	4	4	3	4	3
User6	4	4	4	3	3
User7	4	4	3	3	3
User8	4	4	4	3	3
User9	5	4	4	3	4
User10	4	4	4	3	4
Total	41	39	37	32	32
Avg	4.1	3.9	3.7	3.2	3.2

User1 and User2 are Ph.D. students (Computer Science.) User1 is Male and age is 35 and User2 is female, age is 30. User3, User4, User5, and User6 are four post graduate students (Computer Science.). User3 and User5 are male of age group 23, User4 and User6 are female of age group 23. User7 and User8 are two patients with some technical knowledge. User7 is male of age 45 and User8 is female of age 35. User9 and User10 are two patients without technical knowledge. User9 is male of age 65 and User10 is female of age 58.

Since the model is dealing with medical data which is highly sensitive and privacy of patient should be maintained. Any patient will have the feel that their medical data should not be known to others and medical diagnosis should be reliable. So protecting medical data is very important. Hence data security and reliability is included in the questionnaire.

By explaining the prototype of this model and giving essential information about the working principles of this model patient can know where the system has security or not. End-user can judge the reliability if their data is sent without any error to the healthcare center. Also, the privacy of patient is maintained by using patient id and not revealing more details to others even when read by others. Only the authorized doctors or healthcare practioners can view the medical data and interpret the medical data.

4.7   CONCLUSION

In this work, a novel Wearable Personal Healthcare and Emergency alert and tracking system, namely WHEATS is proposed. The proposed system gives flexibility to the users to move freely wherever they wish to go. Existing system restricts user from moving freely outside home because of recording of vital signals setup in home. In case of emergency user is tracked by WHEATS and treatment is given immediately so that user is safe.

WHEATS continuously collects personal health status and periodically sends the status reports to healthcare centre and rapidly issues the alerts for medical aid in case of emergency. WHEATS automatically dial family members, friends, neighbor and ambulance number in case of emergency.

Early diagnosis and disease prevention and medical decision can also be done effectively by using this proposed system. By using this system there is obvious benefit to person to achieve an enhanced quality of life. Once the technology is implemented completely, medical costs will be reduced.

CHAPTER 5

A SECURE TAMPER RESISTANT PRESCRIPTION RFID ACCESS CONTROL SYSTEM

In this chapter the security of a tamper resistant prescription RFID access control system is analyzed. Detailed analysis shows that since reader and tag are devices there is a possibility for mishandling these devices earlier discussed protocol doesn't address this issue. An improved version of the protocol is discussed.

5.1 INTRODUCTION

Patient safety is an important factor for quality of health care. "To Err is Human", in USA adverse events are the third largest cause of death (Kohn et al. 1999). An adverse event is any untoward medical occurrence in a patient or clinical investigation subject administered a pharmaceutical product and which does not necessarily have a causal relationship with this treatment. Adverse events appears during the prescription or validation or dispensation or administration of medication to the patient. Growth of wireless communication technologies changed the traditional healthcare monitoring setup to dynamic monitoring setup environment.

Radio Frequency Identification (RFID) is a wireless technology helps pervasive healthcare environment to perform various tasks such as identifying or tracking patients, reducing medical errors, reducing malicious attacks, measuring patient care and waiting times, monitoring doses of medication, ensure the correct matching between the patient and doctor. Radio Frequency Identification can also be used for various applications such as Retail, supply chain management in wholesale stores, library access control, tolls payments, theft prevention, animal tracking, human implants, e-passports and e-health (Safkhani et al. 2012).

5.2   BIOMETRIC PALM VEIN TECHNOLOGY

Forging palm vein is very difficult and it is hygienic and highly accurate. Palm vein based healthcare record would enable patient as well as the doctors to be authenticated and communications are to be secured and provide good solutions for implementing strong security, differential access to data and definitive audit trials during emergency circumstances (Heathfield et al. 1997).

Palm vein is unique (Figure 5.1). Nobody in this world has the same palm vein. There is no chance for duplication. Hence, validated patient identity can be linked to a healthcare organization's medical records. Human's pattern of blood veins is unique to every individual. Palms have a broad and complicated vascular pattern and thus hold a wealth of differentiating features for personal identification. Also, it will not vary during the person's lifetime. It is a much secured method of authentication and verification because; this blood vein pattern lies under the skin. This makes it almost impossible for others to read or copy (Karthikeyan & Sukanesh 2012).

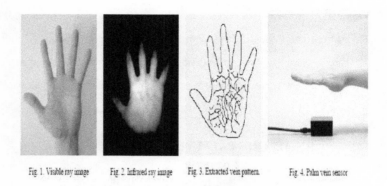

Fig. 1. Visible ray image   Fig. 2. Infrared ray image   Fig. 3. Extracted vein pattern   Fig. 4. Palm vein sensor

Figure 5.1 Palm vein and scanner image

An individual first rests his wrist, and on some devices, the middle of his fingers, on the sensor's supports such that the palm is held centimeters above the device's scanner, which flashes a near-infrared ray on the palm. Unlike the skin, through which near-infrared light passes, deoxygenated hemoglobin in the blood flowing through the veins absorbs near-infrared rays, illuminating the hemoglobin, causing it to be visible to the scanner. Arteries and capillaries, whose blood contains oxygenated hemoglobin, which does not absorb near-infrared light, are invisible to the sensor. The still image captured by the camera, which photographs in the near-infrared range, appears as a black network, reflecting the palm's vein pattern against the lighter background of the palm.

An individual's palm vein image is converted by algorithms into data points, which is then compressed, encrypted, and stored by the software and registered along with the other details in his profile as a reference for future comparison. Then, each time a person logs in attempting to gain access by a palm scan to a particular bank account or secured entryway, etc., the newly captured image is likewise processed and compared to the registered one or to the bank of stored files for verification, all in a period of seconds.

Numbers and positions of veins and their crossing points are all compared and, depending on verification, the person is either granted or denied access.

On the basis of testing the technology on more than 70,000 individuals, it is declared that the new system had a false rejection rate of 0.01% (i.e., only one out of 10,000 scans were incorrect denials for access), and a false acceptance rate of less than 0.00008% (i.e., incorrect approval for access in one in over a million scans). Also, if your profile is registered with your right hand, don't log in with your left – the patterns of an individual's two hands differ (Lee 2012). And if you registered your profile as a child, it'll still be recognized as you grow, as an individual's patterns of veins are established in utero (before birth). No two people in the world share a palm vein pattern – even those of identical twins differ (so your evil twin won't be able to draw on your portion of the inheritance!).

5.3 ELECTRONIC HEALTH RECORD

Nowadays target of RFID technology is Health Sector. Carrying and maintaining medical records should be reduced for elders and patients who face difficultly in carrying medical records to hospital. Prescription given by the doctor can be saved in hospital database server and through RFID tag; data can be retrieved by the doctor whenever the patient is coming to the hospital for treatment.

Electronic health record (EHR) system authority of readers should be different for accessing different data. To improve the patients' safety, reduce altered or forged prescriptions, and deter drug abuse the tamper resistant prescription issue has been considered in Canada and United States (Chen et al. 2012). To address this requirement, recently (Chen et al. 2012)and (Safkhani et al. 2012) have proposed a novel (claimed to be) tamper resistant prescription RFID access control protocol for different authorized readers.

Tamper-resistant prescription requirements with Effect from April 1, 2008, will require that all Medicaid prescription blanks incorporate at least one of the characteristics listed below. To be considered tamper resistant after October 1, 2008, prescription blanks must include all three of the following characteristics (Chen et al. 2012):

- One or more industry-recognized features designed to prevent unauthorized copying of a completed or blank prescription form

- One or more industry-recognized features designed to prevent the erasure or modification of information written on the prescription by the prescriber and

- One or more industry-recognized features designed to prevent the use of counterfeit prescription forms.

Tamper resistant prescription RFID access control system should be designed for medical data because data is very sensitive. By using this prescription maintaining and carrying medical records is reduced for elders and patients. Every medical record is stored in hospital database server as E-record. So by this way maintaining paper records and paper usage is reduced. Thus environment friendly approach can be maintained in hospital environment setup.

5.4   PRELIMINARIES

Notations used in this work are as follows, some of them are similar to the notations used in (Chen et al. 2012) and (Masoumeh et al. 2012) :

PVR   -   palm vein of reader

PVP   -   palm vein of patient

PVPT   -   palm vein of patient wearing tag

RPV   -   reader patient verification

F_i -   flag

Key_S -   key of the back-end database.

Key_T -   key of the tag.

Key_R -   key of the reader which is assigned as $Key_R = h(Key_S, ID_R)$.

ID_T -   the identifier of the tag.

ID_R -   the identifier of the reader.

DID_T -   Dynamic identifier of tag

HID_T -   the pseudonym identifier of the tag, i.e., hash value of the tag's ID_T which is used as the primary index of the prescriptions database to retrieve the tag's key Key_T.

Asc_{RT} -   the required proof to confirm that the current reader has the authority to access the tag, which is generated as $Asc_{RT} = h(Key_T, Key_R)$ and stored in the tag only.

Asc_{PVPT} - the required proof to confirm that the current patient has the authority to use the tag, which is generated as $Asc_{PVPT} = h(Key_T, Key_{PVP})$ and stored in the tag only.

P_i -   the patient's i^{th} prescription recorded by the back-end database.

HP_i -   the pseudonym value of prescription P_i, which is determined as $HP_i = h(P_i)$.

HC_i -   the prescription's hash chain, which is computed as $h(P_{i-1}, P_i)$.

$\oplus$ -   Exclusive OR operation.

$h(.)$ -   the one-way hash function.

$E_K(.)$ -   a symmetric encryption function which uses K to encrypt the message.

$D_K(.)$ -   a symmetric decryption function which uses K to decrypt the message.

N_X -   Random number generated by a protocol party.

$X|a \sim b$ -   A fraction of string X includes bit b to bit a, where $a > b$.

5.5   SECURITY ANALYSIS

5.5.1   Security Analysis of Chen et al..'s Protocol

Impersonating a legitimate doctor in protocol of Chen et al.. Chen et al. claims that their protocol is resistant against the spoofed reader attacks. More precisely, the authors state that to impersonate the reader, the adversary should generate a valid h (Key_R, N_{T_2}), where Key_R is a secret parameter.

All proposed attacking techniques against Chen et al..'s are in light of the following Vulnerabilities of the protocol:

- In each authentication, the back-end database does not contribute to the protocol randomness, which obviously made the protocol vulnerable to reader-to-server (back-end database) impersonation.

- The protocol messages are not carefully scrutinized and, in each authentication, the generated messages by the tag do not employ the generated random numbers symmetrically and it is possible to change a part of the tag's response while the rest of the response remains valid.

- The reader does not employ all random values injected by the tag in the protocol.

- The back-end database does not employ all random values injected by the tag in its feedback to the tag.

Figure 5.2 shows the authentication phase of chen et al.'s protocol.

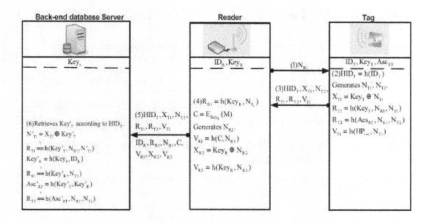

Figure 5.2   The authentication phase of Chen et al..'s protocol (Chen et al. 2012)

5.5.2   Security Analysis of Safkhani et al.'s Protocol

Even though server does verification between reader and tag, there is a possibility for mishandling or interchanging tag and reader knowingly or unknowingly. Since only devices are authenticated not the user using these devices. So there is a chance for any active adversary can impersonate the doctor efficiently and access the tag. Figure 5.3 shows the authentication phase of Safkhani et al.'s protocol.

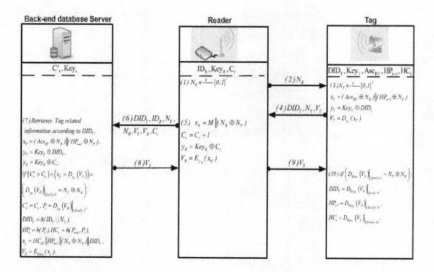

Figure 5.3   The authentication phase of Safkhani et al..'s protocol (Safkhani et al. 2012)

5.6   PROPOSED PROTOCOL

If tag is mishandled or interchanged knowingly or unknowingly any active adversary can impersonate the doctor efficiently and access the tag. Hence if reader wants to access the tag, reader has to send palm vein scanned to the server for verification along with tag wearer palm vein. Our work mainly focuses on right treatment for right patient by right doctor. Previous protocol chen et al.'s and Safkhani et al.'s verification are not sufficient to avoid malicious attacks. Next, we exhibit an improved version of protocol for multiple reader scenario which is more efficient compared to the original protocol while provides the desired security against the presented attacks.

Scenario1: if a diabetic patient is expected to do an eye surgery. Patient must take advice from diabetes doctor. So Reader A (doctor) has to refer another Reader B (doctor) for further treatment. Previous protocol designed is not suitable for this scenario.

Scenario 2: Reader and tag are devices. Association between them is verified by the server or database. But the user who is using these devices is not verified. So there is possibility for malicious user to use these devices. Previous protocol designed is not suitable for this scenario.

Proposed protocol uses palm vein technology for authentication of reader and tag user. There is no possibility for adversary to attack. Hence it is safe compared to existing chen et al.'s and Safkhani et al.'s protocols. Also for scenario like if patient wants to meet other doctor for further treatment without any problem our protocol takes care by introducing flag value and palm vein of all doctor. So patient treatment can be tracked and adversary can be avoided.

5.6.1   The Authentication Phase

Since a doctor uses his reader to access his patient's tag, the reader and the tag should be authenticated by the back-end database server. Also, the reader and tag users' palm vein should also be authenticated. The procedure for this phase is discussed as below:

Reader to Tag

Step 1: The reader generates a random number N_{R_1}, PVR_1 and PVP then emits this number to the tag.

$$N_{R_1} \overset{s}{\leftarrow} \{0,1\}^l, PVR_1 \overset{s}{\leftarrow} \{0,1\}^l, \text{RPV} = E_{Y_R}(PVP)$$

From reader to tag N_{R_1}, PVR_1 and RPV is sent.

Tag to Reader

Step 2: Tag sends DID_T, N_T, V_T to reader.

$$N_T \overset{s}{\leftarrow} \{0,1\}^l$$

$$X_T = (Asc_{RT} \oplus N_{R_1} \oplus PVR_1) \parallel (Asc_{PVPT} \oplus HP_{i-1} \oplus N_T \oplus RPV)$$

$$Y_T = Key_T \oplus DID_T$$

$$V_T = D_{Y_T}(X_T)$$

Reader to Server

Step 3: Reader sends $DID_T, ID_{R_1}, N_T, N_{R_1}, V_T, V_R, C^1{}_r$ to server.

$$X_R = M \parallel (N_{R_1} \oplus N_T) \parallel F_i \parallel ID_{R_2}$$

$$C^1{}_r = C^1{}_r + 1$$

$$Y_R = Key_R \oplus C^1{}_r$$

Flag F_i value is set by reader and sent to server. If F_i is zero there is no need to refer to another doctor. Otherwise another doctor should be referred and tag should be associated to reader2.

Server to Reader

Step 4: Server sends V_S to reader retrieves tag related information according to DID_T

$$X_T = (Asc_{RT} \oplus N_{R_1} \oplus PVR_1) \| (HP_{i-1} \oplus N_T)$$

$$Y_T = Key_T \oplus DID_T$$

$$Y_R = Key_R \oplus C_r$$

$$if(C^1{}_r > C_r) \wedge (X_T = D_{Y_T}(V_T)) \wedge (D_{Y_R}(V_R) | (1\text{-}1) \sim 0 = N_T \oplus N_{R_1}):$$

$$C^1{}_r = C_r , P_i = D_{Y_R}(V_R) | (2l\text{-}l) \sim 1$$

$$DID_T = \text{h}(ID_T \| N_T$$

$$HP_i = \text{h}(P_i), HC_i = h(P_{i-1}, P_i)$$

$$\text{if}(F_i == 0)$$

$$X_s = HC_{i_R} \| HP_{i-1} \| (N_T \oplus N_{R_1}) \| DID_T$$

$$V_s = E_{Key_T}(X_s)$$

Else

$$X_s = HC_{i_R} \| HP_{i-1} \| (N_T \oplus N_{R_1}) \| DID_T \| Asc_{R2T} \| PVR_1$$

$$V_s = E_{Key_T}(X_s)$$

Reader to Tag

Step 5: Reader sends Vs to tag.

Step 6: Tag after receiving Vs

$$\text{if}(D_{keyT}(V_S) | (2l - l)\sim 1 = N_T \oplus N_{R_1}):$$

$$DID_T = D_{keyT}(V_S)|(1\text{-}1) \sim 0$$

$$H_{P_{i-1}} = D_{keyT}(V_S)|(3\text{l-}1) \sim 21$$

$$H_{C_i} = D_{keyT}(V_S)|(4l - l) \sim 31$$

Step 7: Continue the above process from step1 if flag value is not equal to zero.

5.7 CONCLUSION

In this work the security of a tamper resistant prescription RFID access control system is analyzed. Detailed analysis shows that since reader and tag are devices there is a possibility for mishandling these devices earlier discussed protocol doesn't address this issue. In earlier protocol only devices are authenticated not user who is using or going to use. This leads to malicious attacks with the success probability is '1' and the complexity of the learning phase of the attack is only eavesdropping a part of one run of the protocol. Surprisingly, our adversary can force the back-end database to change the patient's prescription to any prescription which has been already prescribed by the same doctor to a patient, while the adversary was there. This property of the protocol puts the patient safety on risk and it is enough to reject the practical usage of this protocol.

Finally, although designing of a secure biometric palm vein technology based RFID access control sounds to not be closed yet. An improved version of the protocol is presented in this work.

CHAPTER 6

A SECURE READER TO READER COMMUNICATION

In this chapter the importance of reader to reader communication is explained with scenarios and authentication mechanism for reader to reader communication is discussed.

6.1   INTRODUCTION

In this work, a secure RFID (radio frequency identification) reader to reader communication using chaos based key exchange protocol for tamper resistant prescription RFID Access control system is discussed. Proposed approach may be the first approach towards RFID reader to reader communication. Also, a scenario where reader to reader communication is very important is discussed.

6.2   TAMPER RESISTANT PRESCRIPTION

Tamper-resistant prescription requirements with Effect from April 1, 2008, will require that all Medicaid prescription blanks incorporate at least one of the characteristics listed below. To be considered tamper resistant after October 1, 2008, prescription blanks must include the following characteristics (Chen et al. 2012):

- Industry-recognized features one or more should be designed to prevent unauthorized copying of a completed or blank prescription form; the erasure or modification of information written on the prescription by the prescriber; and the use of counterfeit prescription forms.

- Medical data is very sensitive. So, there is need for tamper resistant prescription. Maintaining and carrying medical records are reduced for elders and patients by designing Tamper resistant prescription RFID access control system.

- Hospital database server stores every medical record as electronic record. So by this way, paper records and paper usage are eliminated. Thus, hospital will be environment friendly.

6.3 CRYPTOSYSTEM BASED ON CHEBYSHEV POLYNOMIALS

Chebyshev polynomials are public key cryptosystem. It is a generalization of the ElGamal public-key cryptosystem and which was proposed in (Kocarev & Tasev 2003). (Bergamo et al. 2005) discussed about Chebyshev polynomials floating point implementation and the security analysis.

Cryptosystems (Chebyshev Polynomials)

Key Generation algorithm, an Encryption algorithm, and a Decryption algorithm are the three algorithms used in cryptosystems. These algorithms are discussed below: Key Generation Algorithm: for Key generation three steps are needed as below: Reader1, for keys generation, does the following:

- Generates a large integer a.

- Selects a random number x $\in$[-1, 1] and computes Ta(x).

- Reader1 sets his public key to (x, Ta(x)) and his private key to a.

Encryption Algorithm: for Encryption five steps are needed as below:

Reader2, to encrypt a message, does the following operations:

- Obtain Reader1's authentic public key (x, Ta(x)).

- Represents the message as a number M$\in$ [-1, 1].

- Generates a large integer r.

- Computes $T_r(x).T_{r.a}(x)=T_r(Ta(x))$ and $X=M.T_{r.a}(x)$

- Sends the ciphertext C= ($T_r(x)$,X) to Reader1.

Decryption Algorithm: for Decryption two steps are needed as below:

Reader1, does the following operation to recover the plaintext M from the cipher text C, the steps are as follows:

- Uses his private key s to compute $Ta_r=Ta(T_r(x))$.

- Recovers M by computing $M=X/Ta_r(x)$.

6.4   PRELIMINARIES

Notations used in this work are as follows, some of them are similar to the notations used by (Safkhani et al. 2012):

F_i Flag

SC Session close

$HOIDR^*{}_i$ Hand over to id of Reader ith

Key_S The key of the back-end database

Key_T The key of the tag

Key_R The key of the reader which is assigned as $Key_R = h(Key_S, ID_R)$

ID_T The identifier of the tag

ID_R The identifier of the reader

DID_T Dynamic identifier of tag

HID_T The pseudonym identifier of the tag, i.e., hash value of the tag's ID_T which is used as the primary index of the prescriptions database to retrieve the tag's key Key_T

Asc_{RT} The required proof to confirm that the current reader has the authority to access the tag, which is generated as $Asc_{RT} = h(Key_T, Key_R)$ and stored in the tag only

P_i The patient's ith prescription recorded by the back-end database

HP_i The pseudonym value of prescription P_i, which is determined as $HP_i = h(P_i)$

HC_i The prescription's hash chain, which is computed as $h(P_{i-1}, P_i)$

$\oplus$ Exclusive or operation

$h(.)$ The one-way hash function

$E_K (.)$ A symmetric encryption function which uses K to encrypt the message

$D_K (.)$ A symmetric decryption function which uses K to decrypt the message
N_x Random number generated by a protocol party

$X|a \sim b$ A fraction of string X includes bit b to bit a, where $a > b$.

6.5   Safkhani et al.'s PROTOCOL

This protocol deals only with reader to tag and tag to reader and reader to Back-end database server communication. This protocol is not suitable for the scenarios discussed above. (Figure 5.3 shows the Safkhani et al.'s protocol).

6.6   IMPROVED PROTOCOL

An improved version of protocol for reader to reader communication by using key exchange protocol for scenarios presented above is discussed. This is more efficient compared to the previous Safkhani et al.'s protocol. This protocol uses light weight computation key exchange protocol.

The authentication phase

Since a doctor uses his reader to access his patient's tag, the reader and the tag should be authenticated by the back-end database server and also all the readers who have registered in the server. The procedure for this phase is discussed as below:

Reader to Tag

Step 1.   The reader generates a random number N_{R1},

$$N_{R1} \xleftarrow{s} \{0,1\}^1$$

Reader sends N_{R1} to the tag.

Tag to Reader

Step 2.   Tag sends DID_T, N_T, V_T to reader.

$$N_T \overset{s}{\leftarrow} \{0,1\}^1$$

$$X_T = (Asc_{RT} \oplus N_{R1} \parallel HP_{i=1} \oplus N_T)$$

$$Y_T = key_T \oplus DID_T$$

$$V_T = D_{Y_T}(X_T)$$

Reader to Server

Step 3.   Reader sends DID_T, ID_{R1},N_T,N_{R1},V_T,V_R,C_r to server.

$$X_R = M \parallel (N_{R_1} \oplus N_T) \parallel Fi \parallel HOIDR^*{}_i)$$

$$C_r = C_r + 1$$

$$Y_R = key_R \oplus C_r$$

$$V_R = E_{Y_R}(X_R)$$

Flag F_i value is set by reader and sent to the server.   if F_i is zero there is no need to refer to another doctor.   Otherwise handover is required and tag should be associated with next reader.

Server to Reader1

Step 4.   Server sends V_S to reader

Retrieves tag related information according to DID_T

$$X_T = (Asc_{RT} \oplus N_{R1}) \parallel (HP_{i-1} \oplus N_T)$$

$$Y_T = key_T \oplus DID_T$$

$$Y_R = key_R \oplus C_r$$

$$if(C^1{}_r > C_r) \wedge (X_T = D_{Y_T}(V_T)) \wedge (D_{Y_R}(V_R) \mid (1-1) \sim 0 = N_T \oplus N_{R_1}):$$

$$C^1_r = C_r, P_i = D_{Y_R}(V_R) \mid (2l\text{-}l) \sim 1$$

$$DID_T = h\ (ID_T \parallel N_T$$

$$HP_i = h(P_i),\ HC_i = h(P_{i-1}, P_i)$$

if $(F_i == 0)$

$$X_s = HC_{i_R} \parallel HP_{i-1} \parallel (N_T \oplus N_{R_1}) \parallel DID_T$$

$$V_s = E_{key_T}(X_s)$$

Else

Server generates $x \in [-1, 1]$ sends to reader 1 as $KR_1(x)$ and reader2 as $KR_2(x)$.

Reader1 computes $T_S(x)$ and Reader2 computes $T_r(x)$ where $K=T_{rs}(x)$.

Using K both reader1 and reader2 does the key exchange through server.

Server to Reader2

$$X_s = HC_{i_R} \parallel HP_{i-1} \parallel (N_T \oplus N_{R_1}) \parallel DID_T \parallel HOIDR^*_i \parallel Asc_{R2T} \parallel SC$$

$$V_s = E_{key\,T}(X_s)$$

If SC value is zero reader1 session is closed and reader2 starts session with tag and server.

Reader to Tag

Step 5. Reader sends V_S to tag

Step 6.   Tag after receiving V_S

$$\text{if } (D_{keyT} \ (V_S)|(2l - l)\sim 1 = \ N_T \ \oplus \ N_{R_1}):$$

$$DID_T = \ D_{keyT}(V_S)|(l\text{-}l) \sim 0$$

$$H_{P_{i-1}} = D_{keyT}(V_S)|(3l\text{-}l) \sim 2l$$

$$H_{C_i} = \ D_{keyT} \ (V_S)|(4l - l)\sim 3l$$

Step 7.   Continue the above process from step1 if flag value is not equal to zero.

Security analysis of the improved protocol

For the scenarios discussed above if patient wants to meet other doctor for further treatment without any problem our protocol takes care by introducing flag value and session close. So therefore patient treatment can be tracked and adversary can be avoided.

Resistance against reader impersonation attack

Since flag value shows the reader status this value is stored in server which can prevent reader impersonation attack.

6.7   CONCLUSION

In this work, first key exchange protocol for secure reader to reader communication is proposed. If patient wants to be treated by other doctor existing protocol is not suitable for this scenario. Finally, although designing of a secure reader to reader communication by using key exchange protocol RFID access control sounds to be not closed yet, an improved version of the protocol which is much efficient is presented.

CHAPTER 7

CONCLUSION AND FUTURE ENHANCEMENTS

7.1   CONCLUSION

This thesis has made an attempt to improve the patients' care, quality of life, maintain patients' identity and address emergency issues by using pervasive healthcare systems. Also, some of the pervasive healthcare systems issues like energy management in devices, security of medical data, identification of patients, accessing techniques of electronic health record and efficient resource management are solved by proposing new model and protocol. The unique feature of this research work is that it covers some parts of pervasive healthcare systems which is very important for wellness and personalized care of the patients when they are inside or outside the hospital. Devices used in pervasive healthcare systems are very limited in energy resources. In this work ways to improve energy efficiency, to reduce adverse events and to reduce patient misidentification is done and results shows that there is slight improvement in this attempt compared to existing methods in this field.

Simulation results show that the Reselection of cluster heads has better energy efficiency when compared with LEACH, W-LEACH, E- LEACH, and LEACH-FL. Also, by using min heap algorithm load balancing among cluster heads is done to improve energy efficiency still further. Simulation results show that an integration of WBANs and WSNs application can improve quality of life for the patient. Wearable personal healthcare and emergency alert and tracking system helps to achieve an enhanced quality of life. As a proof-of-concept the proposed model is better than existing models.

A Secure protocol for accessing patient electronic health record using palm vein which is unique in nature can prevent from malicious attacks and unauthorized reader usage which in turn ensures patient safety. Reader to reader communication protocol is designed using key exchange protocol. This protocol helps in multiple reader communication and reader to reader communication. Hence patient can be treated in an effective manner. Also, by using wireless sensor network, wireless body area network and radio frequency identification, qualitative treatment to patients is ensured.

7.2   FUTURE ENHANCEMENTS

There are a number of directions available for an extension of this research work. Some of the questions and methods still to be explored in the research work are as follows:

- Integrating WBAN, WSN and RFID application can open new area of challenges to be addressed in the pervasive healthcare systems.

- In an indoor and outdoor monitoring area of hospital using these integrated applications or devices can lead to a lot of issues like security, privacy, energy management and accessing methods problems which in turn leads to innovation of new methods, algorithms and protocols in this field.

- Trusting of devices used in pervasive healthcare systems should be improved.

- Patent privacy and safety should be ensured.

- Improving patient quality of life should be ensured.

- Noise reduction in data recordings of WSN and WBAN.

REFERENCES

1. Abadi, M & Needham, R 1996, 'Prudent Engineering Practice for cryptographic protocols', IEEE Transactions on Software Engineering, vol. 22, pp. 6-15.

2. Abbasi, AA & Younis, M 2007, 'A Survey on Clustering Algorithms for Wireless Sensor Networks', Computer Communications, vol. 30, no. 1, pp. 2826-2841.

3. Abdulsalam, HM & Ali, BA 2013, 'W-LEACH Based Dynamic Adaptive Data Aggregation Algorithm for Wireless Sensor Networks', International Journal of Distributed Sensor Networks, vol. 2013, pp. 1-11.

4. Agarwal, A, Bansal, N & Gupta, S 2013, 'Peer to Peer Networking and Applications', International Journal of Advanced Research in Computer Science and Software Engineering, vol. 3, no. 8, pp. 578-586.

5. Ahluwalia, P, Gimpel, G & Varshney, U 2015, 'ICT interventions impacting big societal challenges: an electronic healthcare approach to homelessness', International Journal of Electronic Healthcare (IJEH), vol. 8, no. 2/3/4, pp. 95-120.

6. Ahmad, T & Feng, YT 2012, 'An Improved Accelerated Frame Slotted ALOHA (AFSA) Algorithm for Tag Collision in RFID', International Journal of Mobile Network Communications and Telematics (IJMNCT), vol. 2, no. 4, pp. 1-8.

7. Akkaya, K & Younis, M 2005, 'A Survey on Routing Protocols in Wireless Sensor Networks', Ad Hoc Networks, vol. 3, pp. 325-349.

8. Akyildiz, IF, Su, W, Sankara Subramaniam, Y & Cayirci, E 2002, 'Wireless Sensor Networks: a survey', Computer Networks, vol. 38, pp. 393-422.

137

9. Alam, S & De, D 2014, 'Analysis of security threats in wireless sensor network', International Journal of Wireless and Mobile Networks, vol. 6, no.2, pp. 35-46.

10. Alemdar, H & Ersoy, C 2010, 'Wireless Sensor Networks for healthcare: A Survey', Computer Networks, vol. 54, no. 15, pp. 2688-2710.

11. Ameen, MAI & Kwak, KS 2011, 'Social Issues in Wireless Sensor Networks with Healthcare Perspective', The International Arab Journal of Information Technology, vol. 8, no. 1, pp. 52-58.

12. Ameer Ahamed Abbasi & Mohamad Younis 2007, 'A Survey on clustering algorithms for wireless sensor networks', Computer Communications, vol. 30, no. 1, pp. 2826-2841.

13. Aminian, M & Naji, HR 2013, 'A hospital healthcare monitoring system using wireless sensor networks ', Journal of Health and Medical Informatics, vol. 4, no. 2, pp. 1-6.

14. Amit, R, Randeep, S & Abhishilpa, N 2016, 'Wireless Sensor Network - Challenges and Possibilites', International Journal of Computer Applications, vol. 140, no. 2, pp. 1-15.

15. Ananthi, S, Vignesh, V, Hariprakash, R & Padmanabhan, K 2016, 'Remote monitoring of the heart condition of athletes by measuring the cardiac action potential propagation time using a wireless sensor network', International Journal of Engineering and Technology Innovation, vol. 6, no. 2, pp. 123-134.

16. Andrés, AJM, Remón, AC, Burillo, VJ & López, RP 2005, 'EStudio Nacional Sobre los Efectos Advero S ligados a la Hospitalización, ENEAS 2005 Madrid: Ministerio de Sanidad yconsumo, 2006. Consultada el 17 de Diciembre de 2011, en http://www.Seguridaddel paciente.es/contenidos/castellano/2006/ENEAS.pdf.

17. Anliker, Urs, Ward, JA, Lukowicz, P, Tröster, G, Dolveck, F, Baer, M, Keita, F, Schenker, EB, Catarsi, FC, Coluccini, L, Belardinelli, A, Shk larski, D, Alon, M, Hirt, E, Schmid, R & Vuskovic, M 2004, 'AMON: A Wearable Multiparameter Medical Monitoring and Alert System', IEEE Transactions on Information Technology in BioMedicine, vol. 8, no. 4, pp. 415-427.

18. Anrich, B, Mayora, O, Bardram, J & Troster, G 2010, 'Pervasive Healthcare Paving the way for a Pervasive, user-centered and Preventive Healthcare Model', Methods inf med, vol. 49, pp. 67-73.

19. Anton, SR & Sodano, HA 2007, 'A review of Power Harvesting Using Piezoelectric Materials (2003-2006)', Smart Materials and Structures, vol. 16, no. 3, pp. R1-R21.

20. Arora, S, Venkataraman, V, Donohue, S, Biglan, KM, Dorsey, ER, & Little, MA 2014, 'High accuracy discrimination of parkinson's disease participants from healthy controls using smart phones', IEEE International Conference on Acoustics, Speech and Signal Processing (ICASSP), Florence Italy: IEEE, pp. 3641-3644.

21. Asada, HH, Shaltis, P, Reisner, A, Rhee, S & Hutchinson, RC 2003, 'Mobile Monitoring with Wearable Photoplethysmographic Biosensors', IEEE Engineering in Medicine and Biology Magazine, pp. 28-40.

22. Asha, PN, Mahalakshmi, T, Archana, S & Lingareddy, SC 2016, 'Wireless Sensor Networks : A Survey on Security threats issues and challenges', International Journal of Computer Science and Mobile Computing, vol. 5, no. 5, pp. 249-267.

23. Avison, D & Young, T 2007, 'Time to Rethink Health care and ICT?', Communications of the ACM, vol. 50, no. 6, pp. 69-74.

24. Avvenuti, M, Baker, C, Light, J, Tulpan, D & Vecchio, A 2010, 'Non-intrusive patient monitoring of Alzheimer's disease subjects using wireless sensor networks', World congress on privacy, security, trust and the management of e-Business, pp. 161-165.

25. Ayoade, J 2006, 'Security Implications in RFID and Authentication Processing Framework', Computers and Security, vol. 25, no. 3, pp. 207-212.

26. Aziz, O, Lo, B, Darzi, A & Yang, GZ 2006, 'in Body Sensor Networks Chapter1. Body Sensor Networks- introduction', Springer-Verlag, London.

27. Bansal, R 2003, 'Coming Soon to a Wal – Mart Near You', Antenna Propagation Magazine, IEEE, vol. 45, pp. 105-106.

139

28. Basmajian, JV & Deluca, C 1985, 'Muscles Alive', 5th ed. Baltimore: Williams & Wilking.

29. Bergamo, P, Arci, DP, Santis, DA & Kocarev, L 2005, 'Security of Public-Key Cryptosystems Based on Chebyshev Polynomials', IEEE Transactions on Circuits and Systems-I: Regular Papers, vol. 52, no. 7.

30. Bhargava, A & Zoltowski, M 2003, 'Senors and Wireless Communication for medical care', In proc.14th International Workshop on Database and Expert systems Applications, pp. 956-960.

31. Booth, P, Frisch, PH & Miodownik, S 2006, 'Application of RFID in an Integrated Healthcare Environment', Proceedings of the 28th IEEE EMBS Annual International Conference, New York City, USA, pp. 117-120.

32. Boric-Lubecke, O & Lubecke, VM 2002, 'Wireless house calls: using communications technology for healthcare and monitoring', IEEE Microwave Magazine, pp. 43-48.

33. Boughanmi, N, Esseghir, M, Merghem-Boulahiar, L & Khoukhi, L 2013, 'Energy efficient aggregation in wireless sensor networks', ICD/ERA, UMR 6279, Troyes university of technology, 12 rue macie curie, 10000 Troyes- Berlin: Springer.

34. Boyinbode, O, Le, H, Mbogho, A, Takizawa, M & Poliah, R 2010, 'A Survey on Clustering Algorithms for Wireless Sensor Networks', 13th International Conference on Network-Based Information Systems, IEEE, pp. 358-364.

35. Burmester, M, demedeiros, B & Motta, R 2008, 'Provably Secure grouping-proofs for RFID Tags', In proceedings of the 8th Smart Card Research and Advanced Applications (CARDIS), LNCS London, UK, pp. 176-190.

36. Cepnik, C, Lausecker, R & Wallrabe, U 2013, 'Review on Electrodynamic Energy Harvesters – A Classification Approach', Micro Machines, vol. 4, pp. 168-196.

37. Chakrabarty, K, Iyengar, SS, Qi, H & Cho, E 2002, 'Grid Coverage for Surveillance and Target Location in Distributed Sensor Networks', IEEE Transactions on Computers, vol. 51, pp. 1448-1453.

38.   Chakraborty, S, Ghosh, SK, Jamthe, A & Agrawal, DP 2013, 'Detecting mobility for monitoring patients with Parkinson's disease at home using RSSI in a wireless sensor network', Procedia Computer Science, vol. 19, pp. 956-961.

39.   Chao, CM & Hsiao, TY 2009, 'Design of structure-free and energy balanced data aggregation in wireless sensor networks', In 11th IEEE international conference on high performance computing and communication, HPCC, pp. 222-229.

40.   Chassin, MMR & Becher, MEC 2002, 'The Wrong Patient', Academy Clinic, vol. 136, pp. 826-833.

41.   Chatzigiannakis, I, Kinalis, A & Nikoletseas, S 2008, 'Efficient Data Propagation Strategies in Wireless Sensor Networks Using a Single Mobile Sink', Computer Communications, vol. 31, no. 5, pp. 896-914.

42.   Chelli, K 2015, 'security issues in wireless sensor networks: attacks and counter measures', proceedings of the world congress on engineering, vol. 1, pp. 1-6.

43.   Chen, K 2013,' 'unequal cluster-based routing protocol in wireless sensor networks', Journal of Networks, vol. 8, no. 11, pp. 2656-2662.

44.   Chen, YY, Huang, DC, Tsai, ML & Jan, JK 2012, 'A design of tamper resistant prescription RFID access control system', Journal of Medical Systems, vol. 36, pp. 2795-2801.

45.   Chen, Z, Chen, Y, Hu, L, Wang, S et al. 2014, 'ContextSense: unobtrusive discovery of incremental social context using dynamic Bluetooth data', in proceedings of the 2014 ACM International Joint Conference on Pervasive and Ubiquitous Computing Adjunct Publication ubicomp'14 Adjunct Seattle USA: ACM Press, pp. 23-26.

46.   Cheng, CY & Chai, JW 2012, 'Deployment of RFID in Healthcare Facilities – Experimental Design in MRI Department', Journal of Medical Systems, vol. 36, pp. 3423-3433.

47.   Cherukuri, Sriram, Venkatasubramanian, KK & Gupta, SK 2003, 'A Biometric Based Approach for Securing Communication Wireless Networks of Biosensors Implanted in Human Body', Proc. of 2003 International Conference on Parallel Processing Workshops (ICCPW'03), pp. 1530-2016.

48. Chien, HY 2006, 'Secure Access Control Schemes for RFID Systems with Anonymity', International Conference on Mobile Data Management, pp. 96-99.

49. Chien, HY, & Liu, SB 2009, 'Tree-based RFID Yoking Proof', In Proceedings of the Conference on Networks, Security, Wireless Communications and Trusted Computing (NSWCT), Hubei, China, pp. 550-553.

50. Chien, HY, Yang,CC, Wu, TC & Lee, CF 2010, 'Two RFID-based solutions to enhance inpatient medication safety', Journal of Medical Systems, vol. 35, pp. 369-375.

51. Cho, JS, Yeo, SS, Hwang, S, Rhee, SY & Kim, SK 2008, 'Enhanced yoking proof protocols for RFID tags and tag groups', In proceedings of the International Conference on Advanced Information Networking and Applications Workshops(AINAW), Okinawa, Japan, pp. 1591-1596.

52. Codagnone, C 2009, 'Reconstructing the whole: Present and future of Personal Health Systems', Deliverable D.6.2 PHS 2020.

53. Colin, W, Mike, G, Frank, W, Rodney, B & Darren, G 2004, 'The Effects of Exercise Intensity and Body Position on Cardiovascular Variables During Resistance Exercise', Journal of Exercise Physiology, vol. 7, no. 4, pp. 29-36.

54. Cook, DJ & Das, SK 2012, 'Pervasive computing at scale: Transforming the state of the art', Pervasive and Mobile Computing, vol. 8, pp. 22-35.

55. Coyle,S et al. 2010, 'BIOTEX- Bio sensing textiles for personalized healthcare management', IEEE Transactions on information technology in Biomedicine, vol. 14, no. 2, pp. 364-370.

56. Crosby, GV, Ghosh, T, Murimi, R & Chin, CA 2012, 'Wireless Body Area Networks for Healthcare: A Survey', International Journal of Adhoc, Sensor and Ubiquitous Computing, vol. 3, no.3, pp. 1-26.

57. Cui, X, Zhang, X & Shang, Y 2007, 'Energy-Saving Strategies of Wireless Sensors Networks', in Proceedings of the IEEE International Symposium on Microwave, Antenna, Propagation and EMC Technologies for Wireless Communications (MAPE'07), pp. 178-181.

142

58. Curone, D et al. 2010, 'Smart garments for emergency operators: The ProeTEXProjectt', IEEE Transactions on information technology and Biomedicine, vol. 14, no. 3, pp. 694-701.

59. Darwish, A & Hassanien, AE 2011, 'Wearable and Implantable Wireless Sensor Network Solutions for Healthcare Monitoring', Sensors'11, DOI: 10.3390/S110605561.

60. Denis, T 2016, 'Wireless Sensors Grouping Proofs for Medical Care and Ambient Assisted- Living Deployment', Sensors Journal, vol. 16, no. 33, pp. 1-12.

61. Dishman, E 2004, 'Inventing Wellness Systems for ageing in Place', Computer, vol. 37, no. 5, pp. 34-41.

62. Domdouzis, K, Kumar, B & Anumba, C 2007, 'Radio-Frequency Identification (RFID) Applications: A Brief Introduction', Advanced Engineering Informatics, vol. 21, pp. 350- 355.

63. Erturk, A & Inman, DJ 2008, 'A Distributed Parameter Electromechanical Model for Cantilevered Piezo Electric Energy Harvesters', Journal of Vibration and Acoustics, vol. 130, no. 4, pp. 1-15.

64. Fan, KW, Liu, S & Sinha, P 2007, 'Structure-free data aggregation in Sensor networks', IEEE Transactions on Mobile Computing, vol. 6, no. 8, pp. 929-942.

65. Fang, D, Hu, J, Wei, X, Shao, H & Luo, Y 2014, 'A smart phone healthcare monitoring system for oxygen saturation and heart rate ', in. proceedings of .International conference cyber-Enabled Distributed Computing Knowledge Discovery (Cyberc), pp. 245-247.

66. Fisher, JA & Monahan, T 2008, 'Tracking The Social Dimensions of RFID Systems in Hospitals', International Journal of Medical Informatics, vol. 77, no. 3, pp. 176-183.

67. Fisher, JA 2006, 'Indoor Positioning and Digital Management: Emerging Surveillance Regimes in Hospitals', In: Mohahan, T. (Ed.) Technological Politics and Power in Everyday Life, pp. 77-88.

68. Gao, X, Xiang, Z, Wang, H, Shen, J, Huang, J & Song, S 2004, 'An Approach to Security and Privacy of RFID System for Supply Chain', The E-Commerce Technology for Dynamic E-Business, pp. 164-168.

69.	Granjal, J, Monteiro, E & Silva, JS 2015, 'Security in the integration of low-power Wireless Sensor Networks with the Internet: A Survey', Ad Hoc Network, vol. 24, pp. 264-287.

70.	Guilar, N, Chen, A, Kleeburg, T & Amivtharajah, R 2006, 'Integrated Solar Energy Harvesting and Storage', in Proceedings of the 11th ACM/IEEE International Symposium on Low Power Electronics and design (ISLPED'06), pp. 20-24.

71.	Gupta, N, Aggrawal, A & Kumar, N 2012, 'Wearable Sensors for Remote Healthcare Monitoring System', International Journal of Engineering Trends and Technology, vol. 3, no. 1, pp. 37-42.

72.	Haahr, RG et al. 2012, 'An electronic patch for wearable health monitoring by reflectance pulse oximetry', IEEE Transactions on Biomedicine and Circuits System, vol. 6, no. 1, pp. 45-53.

73.	Heathfield, HA, Peer, V, Hudson, P, Kay, S, Mackay, L, Marley, T, Nicholson, L, Roberts, R & Williams, J 1997, 'Evaluating Large Scale Health Information Systems: From Practice Towards Theory', in Proceeding AMIA 1997. Philadelphia, PA: Nashville, Hauley and Belfur, Inc., pp. 116-121.

74.	Heinzelman, W, Chandrakasan, A & Balakrishnan, H 2000, 'Energy-Efficient Communication Protocol for Wireless Microsensor Networks', Proceedings of the 33rd International Conference on System Sciences (HICSS'00).

75.	Heinzelman, W, Chandrakasan, A & Balakrishnan, H 2002, 'An Application Specific Protocol Architecture for Wireless Microsensor Networks', IEEE Transactions on Wireless Communications, vol. 1, no. 4, pp. 660-669.

76.	Hoang, DC, Tan, YK, Chng, HB & Panda, SK 2009, 'Thermal Energy Harvesting from Human Warmth for Wireless Body Area Network in Medical Healthcare System', in Proceedings of the International Conference on Power Electronics and Drive Systems (PEDS'09), pp. 1277-1282.

77.	Holzinger, A, Searle, G, Prückner, S, Steinbach – Nordmann, S, Kleinberger, T, Hirt, E & Temnitzer, J 2010, 'Perceived Usefulness Among Elderly People: Experiences and Lessons Learned During the Evaluation of a Wrist Device', Pervasive Health, DOI: 10.4108/ICSTp.

78. Hong, J, Kook, J, Lee, S, Kwon, D & Yi, S 2009, 'T-LEACH: The Method of Threshold-based Cluster Head Replacement for Wireless Sensor Networks', Information System Frontiers, vol. 11, no. 5, pp. 513-521.

79. Husna, JAN & Ku, RK-M 2016, 'Wireless Sensor Network: A Bibliographical survey', Indian Journal of Science and Technology, vol. 9, no. 38, pp. 1-21.

80. IMec, RVS, & Centre, H 2011, 'Energy Harvesting for Wireless Autonomous Sensor Systems', in SENSOR + TEST Conferences, pp. 391-397.

81. Intanagonwiwat, C, Govindan, R & Estrin, D 2000, 'Directed diffusion: a scalable and robust communication paradigm for sensor networks', proceedings of the ACM MobiCom'00, Boston, MA, pp. 56-67.

82. Isaac, RB & Enobong PO 2016,'A REVIEW OF WIRELESS SENSOR NETWORKS: APPLICATIONS, CHALLENGES AND PROSPECTS IN BIOMEDICINE', ARPN JOURNAL OF ENGINEERING AND APPLIED SCIENCES, vol. 11, no. 3, pp. 1830-1839.

83. Jain, PC 2011, 'Wireless Body Area Network for Medical Healthcare', IETE Technical Review, vol. 28, no. 4, pp. 362-371.

84. Jamal, GRA, Hassan, H, Das, A, Ferdous, J & Lisa, SA 2013, 'Generation of Usable Electric Power from Available Random Sound Energy', in Proceedings of the 2nd International Conference on Informatics, Electronics and Vision (ICIEV'13), pp. 1-4.

85. Jambhurkar, PW & Baporikar, V 2015, 'wireless sensor network for heart disease detection using data mining technique', International Journal of innovative research in computer and communication engineering, vol. 3, no. 6, pp. 5947-5953.

86. Jamthe A, Chakraborty, S, Ghosh, SK & Agrawal, DP 2013, 'An implementation of wireless sensor network in monitoring of Parkinson's patients using received signal strength indicator', IEEE International conference on Distributed Computing in Sensor Systems, pp. 442-447.

87. Jeon, BH, Cheng, CY & Prabhu, V 2009, 'Modeling and Analysis of Surgery Patient Identification Using RFID', International Journal of Information Systems Serv Sect., vol. 1, pp. 1-14.

88. Jiang, C, Yuan, D & Zhao, Y 2009, 'Towards Clustering Algorithms in Wireless Sensor Networks – A Survey', WCNC 2009, IEEE, pp. 1-6.

89. Jiang, CJ, Shi, WR, Tang, XL, Wang, P & Xiang, M 2012, 'Energy balanced unequal clustering routing protocol for wireless sensor networks', Journal of software, vol. 23, no.5, pp. 1222-1232.

90. Joo-Hee, P, Jin-An, S & Young – Hwan, O 2005, 'Design and Implementation of an Effective Mobile Healthcare System Using Mobile and RFID Technology In: Enterprise Networking and Computing in Healthcare Industry, 2005 HEALTH COM 2005', Proceedings of 7th International Workshop on 2005, pp. 263-266.

91. Jovanov, E, Milenkovic, A, Otto, C & Groen, PCde 2005, 'A Wireless Body Area Network of Intelligent Motion Sensors for Computer Assisted Physical Rehabilitation, vol. 2, no. 6, pp. 1-10.

92. Juels, A 2004, 'Yoking-Proof's for RFID Tags', In proceedings of the second IEEE Annual Conference on Pervasive Computing and Communications Workshops, Orlando, FL, USA, pp. 138-142.

93. Kalkan, K & Levi, A 2014, 'Key distribution scheme for Peer-to-Peer Communication in Mobile under Water Wireless Sensor Networks', Peer-to-Peer Netw. Appl, vol. 7, pp. 698-709.

94. Kang, K, Bae, C, Lee, J & Han, D 2011, 'UHaS: Ubiquitous Health-assistant System Based on Wearable BioMedical Devices', International Journal of Information Processing and Management, vol. 2, no. 2, pp. 114-126.

95. Kaplan, B 1987, 'The Medical Computing "lag": Perceptions of Barriers to the Application of Computers to Medicine', International Journal of Technology Assessment in Healthcare, vol. 3, pp. 123-126.

96. Kario, K, Yasui, N & Yokol, H 2003, 'Ambulatory Blood Pressure Monitoring for Cardiovascular Medicine', IEEE Engineering in Medicine and Biology Magazine, pp. 81-88.

97.   Karthikeyan, N & Sukanesh, R 2012, 'Cloud Based Emergency Health Care Information Service in India', Journal of Medical Systems, pp. 1-6, DOI: 10.1007/S10916-012-9875-6.

98.   Kaur, J & Kaur, T 2014, 'A Comparative Study of Techniques used in Detection and Prevention of Black Hole Attack in Wireless Sensor Networks', International Journal for Research in Applied Science and Engineering Technology, vol. 2, pp. 87-93.

99.   Kaye, J & Zit Zerberger, T 2006, 'Overview of Healthcare, Disease, and Disability. In: Bardarm. JE, Mihailidis A, Dadong W, editors. Pervasive Computing in Healthcare', CRC Press, pp. 3-20.

100. Ke, WC & Manmeet, MDS 2016, 'Wearable Technology Device Security and Privacy Vulnerability Analysis', International Journal of Network Security and Its Applications (IJNSA), vol. 8, no. 3, pp. 19-30.

101. Khan, MY, Javaid, N, Khan, MA, Javaid, A, Khan, ZA & Qasim, U 2013, 'Hybrid DEEC: Towards Efficient Energy Utilization in Wireless Sensor Networks ', World Applied Sciences Journal, vol. 22, no. 1, pp. 126-132.

102. Kim, HW, Lim, SY & Lee, HJ 2006, 'Symmetric Encryption in RFID Authentication Protocol for Strong Location Privacy and Forward Security, IEEE International Conference on Hybrid Information Technology (ICHIT'06), pp. 718-723.

103. Kim, JM, Park, SH, Han, YJ & Chung, TM 2008, 'CHEF: Cluster Head Election Mechanism Using Fuzzy Logic in Wireless Sensor Networks', ICACT 2008, IEEE, pp. 654-659.

104. Ko, J, Lu, C, Srivastava, MB, Stankovic, JA, Terzis, A & Welsh, M 2010, 'Wireless Sensor Networks for Healthcare', Proceedings of the IEEE, vol. 98, no. 11, pp. 1947-1960.

105. Kocarev, L & Tasev, Z 2003, 'Public-Key Encryption Based on Chebyshev Maps', IEEE International Symposium on Circuits and Systems, ISCAS 2003, Bangkok. Thailand, May 25-28.

106. Kohn, LT, Corrigan, JM & Donaldson, MS 1999, 'To err is Human: Building a Safer Health System', Institute of Medicine, National Academy Press, Washington, DC.

147

107. Koop, EC, Mosher, R, Kun, L, Geiling, J, Grigg, E, Long, S, Macedonia, C, Ronald, C, Richard, MS & Rosen, JM 2008, 'Future Delivery of Healthcare: Cybercare', IEEE Engineering in Medicine and Biology Magazine, vol. 27, no. 6, pp. 29-38.

108. Korhonen, I, Parkka, J & VanGils, M 2003, 'Health Monitoring in the home of the future', Engineering in Medicine and Biology Magazine, vol. 22, no. 3, pp. 66-73.

109. Koshima, H & Hoshen, J 2000, 'personal locator services emerge', IEEE Spectrum, pp. 41-48.

110. Krishnamachari, B 2006, 'Networking Wireless Sensors', Cambridge University Press.

111. Ku, CY, Ho, YF & Chang, YW 2006, 'The Implementation of Signing e-documents by Using the Wireless Identity Module of Cellular Phones', International Journal of Mobile Communications, vol. 4, no. 6, pp. 743-760.

112. Kuilab, P & Jana, PK 2012, 'Energy Efficient Load- Balanced Clustering Algorithm for Wireless Sensor Networks', ICCCS-2012, vol. 6, pp. 771-777.

113. Kulik, J, Heinzelman, WR & Balakrishnan, H 2002, 'Negotiation based protocols for disseminating information in wireless sensor networks', Wireless Networks, vol. 8, pp. 169-185.

114. Kulkarni, P & Ozturk, Y 2011, 'mPHASiS: Mobile Patient Healthcare and Sensor Information System', Journal of Network and Computer Applications, vol. 34, no. 1, pp. 402-417.

115. Kumar, V, Jain, A & Barwar, PN 2014, 'Wireless Sensor Networks: Security Issues, Challenges and Solutions', International Journal of Information and Computation Technology, vol. 4, no. 8, pp. 859-868.

116. Landt, J 2005, 'The History of RFID', IEEE Potentials, vol. 24, no. 4, pp. 8-11.

117. Lee, JC 2012, 'A Novel BioMetric System Based on Palm Vein Image', Pattern Recognition Letters, vol. 33, pp. 1520-1528.

118. Lee, LS, Fiedler, KD & Smith, JS 2008, 'Radio Frequency Identification (RFID) Implementation in the Service Sector: A Customer- Facing Diffusion Model', International Journal of Production Economics, vol. 112, pp. 587-600.

119. Lee, SH, Ng, AW & Zhang, K 2007, 'The Quest to Improve Chinese Healthcare: Some Fundamental Issues', International Journal of Healthcare Quality Assurance, vol. 20, pp. 416-428.

120. Leonov, V & Vullers, RJM 2009, 'Wearable Thermoelectric Generators for Body-Powered Devices,' Journal of Electronic Materials, vol. 38, no. 7, pp. 1491-1498.

121. Li, CJ, Liu, L, Chen, SZ, Wu, CC, Huang, CH & Chen, XM 2004, 'Mobile Healthcare Service System Using RFID', Proceedings of IEEE International Conference on Networking, Sensing and Control, Taipei, Taiwan, pp. 1014-1019.

122. Li, H & Tan, J 2010, 'Heartbeat – Driven Medium Access Control for Body Sensor Networks', IEEE Transactions on Information Technology in BioMedicine, vol. 14, no. 1, pp. 44-51.

123. Li, Z & Zhang, G 2007, 'A Physical Activities Healthcare System Based on Wireless Sensing Technology', 13th IEEE International Conference on Embedded and Real-Time Computing Systems and Applications.

124. Liao,Y, Qi, H, & Li ,W 2013, 'Load-balanced clustering algorithm with distributed self-organization for wireless sensor networks', IEEE Sensors Journal, vol. 13, no. 5, pp.1498-1506.

125. Lin, WY, Lee, MY & Chou, WC 2014, 'The design and development of a wearable posture monitoring vest', in proceeding of IEEE International Conference on Consumer Electronics (ICCE), pp. 329-330.

126. Lindsey, S & Raghavendra, CS 2003, 'PEGASIS: Power Efficient Gathering in Sensor Information Systems', Proc. of the IEEE Aerospace Conference, vol. 3, no.1, pp. 1125-1130.

127. Liszka, KJ, Mackin, MA, Lichter, MJ, York, DW, Dilippillai & Rosenbaum, SD 2004, 'Keeping a Beat on the Heart', IEEE Pervasive Computing, vol. 3, pp. 42-49.

128. Liu, X 2012, 'A Survey on Clustering Routing Protocols in Wireless Sensor Networks', Sensors, vol. 12, no. 8, pp. 11113-11153.

129. Loscri, V, Morabito, G & Marano, S 2005, 'A Two-Levels Hierarchy for Low-Energy Adaptive Clustering Hierarchy (TL-LEACH)', VTC-2005-FALL, IEEE, pp. 1809-1813.

130. Lu, E, Lee, HP & Lim, SP 2004, 'Modeling and Analysis of Micro Piezoelectric Power Generators for Micro-electromechanical-Systems Applications', Smart Materials and Structures, vol. 13, no. 1, pp. 57-63.

131. Lymberis, A 2003, 'Smart Wearables for remote health monitoring', from prevention to rehabilitation: current R&D, future challenges', In proc. 4th International IEEE EMBS special topic conference on information technology applications in Biomedicine, pp. 272-275.

132. Malan, D, Fulford-Jones, T, Welsh, M & Moulton, S 2004, 'CodeBlue: An AdHoc Sensor Network Infrastructure for Emergency Medical Care', International Workshop on Wearable and Implantable Body Sensor Networks, DOI: 10.1.1.113.7341.

133. Maskooki, A, Soh, CB, Gunawan, E & Low, KS 2011, 'Opportunistic Routing for Body Area Network', in Consumer Communications and Networking Conference (CCNC), IEEE, pp. 237-241.

134. Matzeu, G, Fay, C, Vaillant, A, Coyle, S :& Diamond, D 2016, 'A wearable device for monitoring sweat rates via image analysis', IEEE transactions on Biomedical Engineering, vol. 63, no. 8, pp. 1672-1680.

135. McCall, WV, 2015, 'A rest-activity biomarker to predict response to SSRIs in major depressive disorder', Journal of Psychiatric Research, vol. 64, pp. 19-22.

136. Mccarthy, JF, Nguyen, DH, Rashid, AM & Soroczak, S 2003, 'Proactive Displays and the Experience Ubicompproject', Adjunct Proceedings of the fifth International Conference on Ubiquitous Computing (UbiComp 2003), 12-15 October 2003, Seattle, pp. 78-81.

137. Meriggi, P et al. 2010, 'Polysomnography in extreme environment the MagIC Wearable System for monitoring climbers at very high altitude on mt. Everest Slopes', in proceeding of Comput. Cardiol, Belfast, North Irland, pp. 1087-1090.

138. Murphy, MF & Kay, JD 2004, 'Patient Identification: Problems and Potential Solutions', Vox Songuinis, vol. 87, pp. 197-202.

139. Najera, P, Lopez, J & Roman, R 2011, 'Real-time location and inpatient care systems based on passive RFID', Journal of Network Computer Applications, vol. 34, pp. 980-987.

140. Neves, PACSN, Stachyra, M & Rodrigues, JR 2008, 'Application of Wireless Sensor Networks to Healthcare Promotion', Journal of Communications Software and Systems (JCOMSS), vol. 4, no. 3, pp. 181-190.

141. Ngai, EWT & Riggins, F 2008, 'RFID: Technology, Applications, and Impact on Business Operations', International Journal of Production Economics, vol. 112, pp. 507-509.

142. Ngai, EWT, Cheng, TCE, AU, S & Lai, K 2007, 'Mobile Commerce Integrated with RFID Technology in a Container Depot', Decision Support Systems, vol. 43, pp. 62-76.

143. Ning, WS, Liang, T & Yuan, YJ 2016, 'Electrocardiography Monitoring System based on Wireless Communications', Journal Southwest Jiaofong Univeristy, vol. 51, no. 1, pp. 193-200.

144. Olivares, A Gorriz, JM, Ramirez, J & Olivares, G 2010, 'A study of Vibration-Based Energy Harvesting in Activities of Daily Living', in Proceedings of the 4th International Conference on Pervasive Computing Technologies for Healthcare (Pervasive Health), vol. 4, pp. 1-4.

145. Østbye, T, Lobach, DF, Cheesborough, D, Lee, AMM, Krause, KM, Hasselblad, V & Bright, D 2003, 'Evaluation of An Infrared/ Radio Frequency Equipment – Tracking System in a Tertiary Care Hospital ', Journal of Medical Systems, vol. 27, pp. 367-380.

146. Oztekin, A, Pajouh, FM, Delen, D & Swim, LK 2010, 'An RFID Network Design Methodology for Asset Tracking in Healthcare', Decision Support Systems, vol. 49, pp. 100-109.

147. Pandian, PS, Safeer, KP, Gupta, P, Shakunthala, DT, Sundershehu, BS & Padaki, VC 2008, 'Wireless Sensor Network for Wearable Physiological Monitoring', Journal of Networks, vol. 3, no. 5, pp. 21-29.

148. Pang,Z, Chen, Q & Zheng, L 2009, 'A Pervasive and Preventive healthcare solution for medication non compliance and daily monitoring', 2nd international symposium on Applied Sciences in Biomedical and Communication Technologies, IEEE, pp. 1-6.

149. Paradiso, JA & Starner, T 2005, 'Energy Scavenging for Mobile and Wireless Electronics', IEEE Pervasive Computing, vol. 4, no. 1, pp. 18-27.

150. Paul, E 2004, 'Reengineering Medication Management from the Bedside Using Bar-coding and Wireless Technology', HIMSS Publication, vol. 1, pp. 61-69.

151. Pedro, PL, Agustin, O, Julio, C & Vanderlubbe, JCA 2010, 'Flaws on RFID Grouping Proofs Guidelines for future sound protocols', Journal of Network Computer Applications, vol. 34, pp. 833-845.

152. Pérez, MM, Canosa, MC, Hermida, JV, Garcia, LC, Gómez, DL, González, GV & Herranz, IM 2012, 'Application of RFID Technology in Patient Tracking and Medication Traceability in Emergency Care', J Med Syst, DOI:10.1007/S10916-012-9871-X.

153. Peris-Lopez, P, Hernanadez-Castro, JC, Estevez-Tapiador, JM & Ribagorda, A 2007, 'Solving the simultaneous scanning problem anonymously: Clumping Proofs for RFID tags', In proceedings of the Security, Privacy and Trust in Pervasive and Ubiquitous Computing (SECPerU), Istanbul, Turkey, pp. 55-60.

154. Peris-Lopez, P, Ortila, A, Mitrokotsa, A, Vanderlubbe, JCA 2011, 'A Comprehensive RFID Solution to enhance inpatient medication safety', Inter. J. Med. Inform, vol. 80, pp. 13-24.

155. Philipp, F, Zhao, P, Samman, EA, Glesner, M, Dassanayake, KB, Maheswararajah, S & Halgamuge, S 2012', Adaptive Wireless Sensor Networks Powered by Hybrid Energy Harvesting for Environmental Monitoring, in proceedings of the IEEE 6th International Conference on Information and Automation for Sustainability (ICIAFS'12), pp. 285-289.

156. Piramuthu, S 2007, 'Protocols for RFID tag/ reader authentication', Decision Support Systems, vol. 43, pp. 897-914.

157. Polson, PG, Lewis, C, Riemapn, J & Wharton, C 1992, 'Cognitive Walkthroughs: A Method for Theory-Based Evaluation of User Interfaces', International Journal of Man- Machine Studies, vol. 36, no. 5, pp. 741-773.

158. Poltavski, DV 2015, 'The use of Single-Electrode Wireless EEG in Biobehavioral investigations ', Mobile Health Technologies: methods in molecular Biology, Springer New York, pp. 375-390.

159. Raatikainen, K, Christensen, H & Nakajima, T 2002, 'Application Requirements for middleware for mobile and pervasive systems', ACM mobile computing and communications Review (MC2R), vol. 6, no. 4, pp. 16-24.

160. Raazi, SMKUR, Lee, H, Lee, S, Lee, YK & BARI+ 2010, 'A Biometric Based Distributed Key Management Approach for Wireless Body Area Networks', Sensors-10, pp. 3911-3933.

161. Rabaey, JM, Ammer, MJ, da Silva Jr, Patel, D & Roundy, S 2000, 'Pico Radio Supports adhoc ultra-low power wireless networking', IEEE Computer Magazine, pp. 42-48.

162. Raskovic, D, Martin, T & Jovanov, E 2004, 'Medical Monitoring Applications for Wearable Computing', The Computer Journal, vol. 47, no. 4, pp. 495-504.

163. Reason, J 2002, 'Combating Omission Errors through Task Analysis and Good Reminders ', Qual. Saf. Healthcare, vol. 11, pp. 40-44.

164. Rieman, MFJ & Redmiles, D 1995, 'Usability Evaluation with the Cognitive Walkthrough CHI '95 Proceedings @ACM'.

165. Roberts, CM 2006, 'Radio Frequency Identification (RFID)', Computers and Security, vol. 25, pp. 18-26.

166. Roundy, S, Wright, PK & Rabaey, J 2003, 'A Study of Low Level Vibrations as a Power Source for Wireless Sensor Nodes', Computer Communications, vol. 26, no.11, pp. 1131-1144.

167. Safkhani, M, Bagheri, N & Naderi, M 2012, 'On the Designing of a Tamper Resistant Prescription RFID Access Control System', J. Med. Syst., DOI: 10.1007/S10916-012-9872-9.

168. Safkhani, M, Bagheri, N & Naderi, M 2014, 'A note on the security of IS-RFID, an inpatient medication safety', Inter. J. Med. Inform, vol. 83, pp. 82-85.

169. Saito, J & Sakurai, K 2005, 'Grouping Proof for RFID Tags', In proceedings of the 19th International Conference on Advanced Information Networking and Applications, Tamkang, Taiwan, pp. 621.

170. Sanchati, R, Minda, K, Hussain, I & Marchya, A 2011, 'A Study and Analysis of Pervasive Computing and its Application', International Journal of Computer Information Systems, vol. 2, no. 5, pp. 44-52.

171. Sandhu, MM, Javaid, N, Akbar, M, Najeeb, F, Qasim, V & Khan, ZA 2014, 'FEEL: Forwarding Data Energy Efficiently with Load Balancing in Wireless Body Area Networks', IEEE 28th International Conference on Advanced Information Networking and Applications, pp. 783-789.

172. Sandulescu, V, Andrew, SS, Ellis, D, Bellotto, N & Mozos, O 2015, 'Stress Detection using Wearable Physiological Sensors', Artificial Computation in Biology and Medicine, vol. 9107 of Lecture Notes in Computer Science, Springer International Publishing, pp. 526-532.

173. Sardouk, A, Mansouli, M, Mergham-Boulahia, L, Gaiti, D & Rahim-Amoud, R 2010, 'Multi-agent system based wireless sensor network for crisis management', In 2010 IEEE global telecommunications conference (GLOBE COM 2010), pp. 1-6.

174. Sarika, Y & Rama, SY 2016, 'A review on energy efficient protocols in Wireless Sensor Networks', Wireless Networks, vol. 22, pp. 335-350.

175. Sasaki, S & Karube, I 1999, 'The Development of Micro fabricated Biocatalytic Fuel Cells', Trends in Biotechnology, vol. 17, no. 2, pp. 50-52.

176. Schepps, J & Rosen, A 2002, 'Microwave industry outlook-wireless communications in healthcare,' IEEE Trans Microwave Theor Tech, vol. 50, no. 3, pp. 1044-1045.

177. Schollmeier, R 2001, 'A Definition of Peer-to-Peer Networking for the Classification of Peer-to-Peer Architectures and Applications', Peer-to-Peer Computing.

178. Schwiebert, L, Gupta, SKS & Weinmenn, J 2001, 'Research Challenges in Wireless Networks of Biomedical Sensors', in 7th Annual International Conference on Mobile Computing and Networking, Rome, Italy, pp. 151-165.

179. Shahriyar, R, Bari, MDF, Kundu, G, Ahamed, SI & Akbar, MDM 2009, 'Intelligent Mobile Health Monitoring System (IMHMS)', International Journal of Control and Automation, vol. 2, no. 3, pp. 13-28.

180. Shang – Wei, W, Wun – Hwa, C, Chorng – Shyong, O, Li, L & Yun-Wen, C 2006, 'RFID Application in Hospitals: A Case Study on A Demonstration RFID Project in a Taiwan Hospital In: System Sciences, HICSS'06', Proceedings of the 39th Annual Hawaii International Conference on 2006, pp. 184a – 184a.

181. Sharma, K & Ghose, MK 2010, 'Wireless Sensor Networks: An overview on its security threats', International Journal of Computer Applications, vol. 8, no. 1, pp. 42-45.

182. Shih, E, Cho, S, ICKes, N, Min, R, Sinha, A, Wang, A & Chandrakasan, A 2001, 'Physical Layer Driven Protocol and Algorithm Design for Energy-Efficient Wireless Sensor Networks', Proceedings of ACM Mobicom'01, Rome, Italy, July 2001, pp. 272-286.

183. Singla, A & Sachdeva, R 2013, 'Review on Security Issues and Attacks in Wireless Sensor Networks', International Journal of Advanced Research in Computer Science and Software Engineering, vol. 3, no. 4, pp. 529-534.

184. Sneha, S & Varshney, U 2013, 'A framework for enabling patient monitoring via mobile ad hoc network', Decision Support Systems, vol. 55, pp. 218-234.

185. Solanas, A & Castella – Roca, J 2008, 'RFID Technology for the Health Care Sector', Recent Pat. Electr. Eng, vol. 1, pp. 22-31.

186. Starner, T 1996, 'Human-powered wearable computing', IBM Systems Journal, vol. 35, no. 3.

187. Sufi, F, Fang, Q, Khalil, I & Mahmoud, SS 2009, 'Novel Methods of Faster Cardiovascular Diagnosis in Wireless Telecardiology', IEEE Journal on Selected Areas in Communications, vol. 27, no. 4, pp. 537-552.

188. Sung, M, Marci, C & Pentland, A 2005, 'Wearable Feedback Systems for Rehabilitation', Journal of Neuro Engineering and Rehabilitation, vol. 2, no. 17, DOI: 10.1186/1743-0003-2-17.

189. Tada , Y, Amano, Y, Sato, T, Saito, S & Inoue, M 2015, 'A smart shirt made with conductive ink and conductive foam for the measurement of electrocardiogram signals with unipolar precordial leads', Fibers, vol. 3, no. 4, pp. 463-477.

190. Taleb, T, Bottazzi, D, Guizani, M & Nait-Charif, H 2009, 'ANGELAH: A Framework for Assisting Elders at Home', IEEE Journal on Selected Areas in Communications, vol. 27, no. 4, pp. 480-494.

191. Tan, YK & Panda, SK 2011, 'Energy Harvesting from Hybrid Indoor Ambient Light and Thermal Energy Sources for Enhanced Performance of Wireless Sensor Nodes', IEEE Transactions on Industrial Electronics, vol. 58, no. 9, pp. 4424-4435.

192. Ting, JSL, Tsang, AHC, Ip, AWH & Ho, GTS 2011, 'RF- Medisys: A Radio Frequency Identification – Based Electronic Medical Record System for Improving Medical Information Accessibility and Services at Point of Care', Health Information Management Journal, vol. 40, pp. 25-32.

193. Ting, L & Yong, JY 2016, 'Wearable Medical Monitoring Systems Based on Wireless Networks: A Review', IEEE SENSORS JOURNAL, vol. 16, no. 23, pp. 8186-8199.

194. Toh, WY, Tan, YK, Koh, WS & Siek, L 2014, 'Autonomous Wearable Sensor Nodes with Flexible Energy Harvesting', IEEE Sensors Journal, vol. 14, no. 7, pp. 2299-2306.

195. Trček, D & Brodnik, A 2013, 'Hard and Soft Security Provisioning for computationally weak pervasive computing systems in e-health', IEEE Wireless Communications, vol. 20, pp. 22-29.

196. Tröster, G 2005, 'The Agenda of Wearable Healthcare. In : IMIA Yearbook of Medical Informatics 2005: Ubiquitous Health Care Systems', Schattauer, pp. 125-138.

197. Tu, YJ, Zhou, W, & Piramuthu, S 2009, 'Identifying RFID – Embedded Objects in Pervasive Healthcare Applications, Decision Support Systems, vol. 46, pp. 586-593.

198.   Tzeng, SF, Chen, WH & Pai, FY 2008, 'Evaluating the Business Value of RFID: Evidence from Five Case Studies', International Journal of Production Economics, vol. 112, pp. 601-613.

199.   Vani, H & Monali, M 2013, 'Security mechanism for wireless sensor network- A review', International Journal on Recent and Innovation Trends in Computing and Communication, vol. 1, no. 12, pp. 915-918.

200.   Varshney, U & Vetter, R 2000, 'Emerging Wireless and Mobile Networks', Communications of the ACM, vol. 43, no. 6, pp. 73-81.

201.   Varshney, U & Vetter, R 2002, 'Mobile Commerce: framework, applications, and networking support,' ACM/Kluwer Mobile Networks and Applications (MONET), vol. 7, no. 3, pp. 185-198.

202.   Varshney, U 2003a, 'The Status and Future of 802.11 Based WLANs,' IEEE Comput, pp. 90-93.

203.   Varshney, U 2003b, 'Location Management for Mobile Commerce Applications in Wireless Internet', ACM Transactions on Internet Technologies, vol.3, no. 3, pp. 236-255.

204.   Varshney, U 2005, 'Pervasive Healthcare: applications, challenges and wireless solutions', communications of the AIS.16, article 3, July.

205.   Varshney, U 2006, 'Using Wireless technologies in healthcare', Int. Journal on Mobile Communications, vol. 4, no. 3, pp. 354-368.

206.   Varshney, U 2007, 'Pervasive Healthcare and Wireless Health Monitoring', Mobile Network Applications, vol. 12, pp. 113-127.

207.   Varshney, U 2014, 'A model for improving quality of decisions in mobile health', Decision Support Systems, vol. 62, pp. 66-77.

208.   Varshney, U 2014, 'Mobile health: Four emerging themes of research', Decision Support Systems, vol. 66, pp. 20-35.

209.   Venkataraman, K, Daniel, JV & Murugaboopathi, G 2013, 'Various Attacks in Wireless Sensor Network: Survey ', International Journal of Soft Computing and Engineering, vol. 3, no. 1, pp. 208-211.

210. Verma, G & Moinuddin 2014, 'Body Area Network – A Perspective', International Journal of Computer Science and Information Technologies, vol. 5, no. 5, pp. 6802-6809.

211. Wang, CC, Chlang, CY, Cin, PY, Chou, C, Kuo, IT, Huang, CN & Chan, CT 2008, 'Development of a fall detecting system for the elderly residents', 2nd international conference on Bioinformatics and Biomedical Engineering, IEEE, pp. 1359-1362.

212. Wang, J, Zuo, L, Zhang, Z, Yang, X & Kim, JU 2013, 'A Reselection-based Energy Efficient Routing Algorithm for Wireless Sensor Networks,' International Journal of Smart Home, vol. 7, no. 4, pp. 1-12.

213. Wararkar, P, Kapil, N, Rehani, V, Mehra, Y & Bhatnagar, Y 2016, 'Resolving Problems Based on Peer to Peer Network Security Issue's', Procedia Computer Science, vol. 78, pp. 652-659.

214. Waterhouse, E 2003, 'New Horizons in Ambulatory Electroencephalography', IEEE Engineering in Medicine and Biology Magazine, pp. 74-80.

215. Watteyne, T, Augé-Blum, I, Dohler, M & Barther, D 2007, 'BodyNets'07: Proceedings of the ICST 2nd International Conference on Body Area Networks', ICST, Article No. 6.

216. Wei, CK & Ramasamy, G 2011, 'A Hybrid Energy Harvesting System for Small Battery Powered Applications', in Proceedings of the IEEE Conference on Sustainable Utilization Development in Engineering and Technology (STUDENT'11), pp. 165-170.

217. Weiya, W & Chao, Li 2009, 'Integrated Application of WBAN and WSN', IEEE fifth International Joint Conference on INC, IMS and IDC, pp. 1884-1888.

218. Wu, F, Kuo, F & Liu, LW 2005, 'The Application of RFID on Drug Safety of Inpatient Nursing Healthcare', ACM International Conference Proceeding Series, pp. 85-92.

219. Wu, W, Cao, J, Zheng, Y & Zheng, YP 2008, 'WAITER: A Wearable Personal Healthcare and Emergency Aid System', Sixth Annual IEEE International Conference on Pervasive Computing and Communications, pp. 680-685, DOI: 10.1109/PERCOM.2008.115.

220. Wu, WH, Bui, AAT, Batalin, MA, Au, LK, Binney, JD & Kaiser, WJ 2008, 'MEDIC: Medical Embedded Device for Individualized Care', Aritifical Intelligence in Medicine, vol. 42, no. 2, pp. 137-152.

221. Xiao, Y, Shen, X, Sun, B & Cai, L 2006, 'Security and Privacy in RFID and Applications in Telemedicine', IEEE Communications Magazine, pp. 64-72.

222. Xiaoling, XU, Shu, L, Guizani, M, Liu, M & Lu, J 2014, 'A Survey on Energy Harvesting and Integrated Data Sharing in Wireless Body Area Networks', Article ID. 438695, pp. 1-17.

223. Xie, R & Jia, X 2014, 'Transmission-efficient clustering method for wireless sensor networks using compressive sensing', IEEE Transactions on Parallel and Distributed Systems, vol. 25, no. 3, pp. 806-815.

224. Yang, BH & Rhee, S 2000, 'Development of the Ring Sensor for Healthcare Automation', Robotics and Autonomus Systems, vol. 30, pp. 273-281.

225. Yang, MT & Huang, SY 2014, 'Appearance-Based Multimodel Human Tracking and Identification for Healthcare in the Digital Home', Sensors, vol. 14, pp. 14253-14277.

226. Yassein, MB, Al-zou'bi, A, Khamayesh, Y & Mardini, W 2009, 'Improvement on LEACH Protocol of Wireless Sensor Network (VLEACH)', International Journal of Digital Content Technology and its Applications, vol. 3, no. 2, pp. 132-136.

227. Younis, O & Fahmy, S 2004, 'HEED: A Hybrid, Energy-Efficient Distributed Clustering Approach for Adhoc Sensor Networks', IEEE Transactions on Mobile Computing, vol. 3, no. 4, pp. 366-379.

228. Yu, F, Park, S, Lee, E & Kim, SH 2010, 'Elastic Routing: A Novel Geographic Routing for Mobile Sinks in Wireless Sensor Networks', IET Commun, vol. 4, no. 6, pp. 716-727.

229. Zahmati, AS, Abolhassani, B, Shirazi, AAB & Bakhtiari, AS 2007, 'An Energy-Efficient Protocol with Static Clustering for Wireless Sensor Networks', International Journal of Computer, Electrical, Automation, Control, and Information Engineering, vol.1, no. 4, pp. 874-877.

CPSIA information can be obtained
at www.ICGtesting.com
Printed in the USA
LVHW110101221122
733724LV00004B/135